The
Political
Criminal

The Political Criminal

The Problem of Morality and Crime

by

Stephen Schafer

THE FREE PRESS
A DIVISION OF MACMILLAN PUBLISHING CO., INC.
New York

COLLIER MACMILLAN PUBLISHERS
London

The Free Press
A Division of Macmillan Publishing Co., Inc.
866 Third Avenue, New York, N.Y. 10022

Collier–Macmillan Canada Ltd.

Library of Congress Catalog Card Number: 73–10700

Printed in the United States of America

printing number
1   2   3   4   5   6   7   8   9   10

To the memory of
LEX

Contents

CONTENTS

Preface

Despite a legion of theories about the crime problem, crime is increasingly with us. In analyzing why laws are criminally violated, most theories contrast crime with justice, many of them contrast crime with morality, but very few seek to explore the relationships between justice and morality in crime. In my search for an answer to the problem of crime I have tried to take my cue from the most striking and perhaps most essential overarching aspect of the vast area of criminal behavior, that is, political criminality, where the complex concept of crime is so provokingly entangled with the concepts of law, justice, and morality.

I realize that any book on the concept of the political criminal would be expected to explore the subject deeply and extensively, since the very existence of the political criminal is considered controversial. The student of political crime for the most part has to work from incomplete or distorted evidence, and any essay on the subject must extend into regions bordering on the limits of comprehension. I apologize for the piecemeal presentation here of so much material in so few pages, and I want to explain this book's uneven and fragmentary coverage. I am not attempting to be comprehensive, nor am I seeking answers to all the problems of political crime.

This long essay should be understood as a body of somewhat abstract statements, in fact more questions than answers, devoid of methodologically fettered and verified empirical study and lacking unification in terms of an all-encompassing theory of crime. It may do only scant justice to the understanding of crime, about which so much has already been written, including both the searchings for truth of brave thinkers as well as some sophisticated nonsense. Much could be said about the vulnerability of many theories of criminal behavior, and I, pressed by the topic of political crime and by issues emanating from it to the general crime problem, have no choice but to extend my skepticism even to my own approach. I would be the first to acknowledge that there can never be a last word on any aspect of man's most tenacious social problem.

It is not possible to express my thanks to all those who have, directly and indirectly, helped me to develop these ideas. I must remember here Professor Paul Angyal who, so many years ago when I was one of his students, called my attention to the significance of political crime in understanding the criminal violation of law. My primary gratitude, however, goes to my late father, who taught me to doubt, without which capacity theoretical speculation may so easily mislead the thinker.

Although I alone am responsible for the orientation of this essay and for the views expressed in it, I wish to acknowledge my thanks to Charles E. Smith of The Free Press for his encouragement and help in bringing my ideas to print, and to Margaret Castagno and George A. Rowland for providing editorial asistance.

Boston, 1973   STEPHEN SCHAFER

The
Political
Criminal

1

The Indestructible Crime Type

Political Crime in History

The political crime is perhaps the oldest of all crime types. It may be that even the celebrated biblical apple-eating was a political act. It is virtually impossible to find a history book of any society which does not record political criminals, those craftsmen of dreams who possess a gigantic reservoir of creative energy as well as destructive force. They have always existed, they exist now, and they will exist in the future in spite of historical experience and the evidence that the ideal is so often destroyed the moment it becomes reality. The ideas and ideals of political criminals are usually feared and resisted not because they are progressive, but because many have proved to be retrograde when once accomplished. Yet when going through the social history of man, we recall most vividly those giants of the past whose political crimes

I

left an indelible imprint. This never-ending stream of political criminals indicates that political crime is no ordinary crime and its history no ordinary history.

Cesare Lombroso, one of the founding fathers of criminology, once suggested that the recurrence of criminal political acts throughout history should be attributed to "misoneism," a hatred or dislike of the new, which dominates every human community, as it does nature. He understood political crime, in its broadest sense, as any action that attacks the legal system, the historical, economic, and social traditions of a society, or any part of the existing social fabric, and which consequently collides with the law.[1] However, this and other definitions of political crime or conceptualizations of "the political criminal," although not always described as such, have been a subject for discussion and argument ever since people began to ask who the heroes of history really were.

In the classical sense, a hero (from the Greek *heros*) signifies a man of great courage, strength, and skill who sometimes possesses supernatural powers, who stands up against destructive monsters, demons, and other ruinous forces, or who excels in wars and exploits against other worlds, sometimes superhuman worlds, or against oppressors who are of his own nation, tribe, or family. From the distant past we have inherited an inspiring and grand body of heroic poetry and saga which narrates the tales of early heroes, those princely characters who made voyages of discovery, participated in intertribal warfare and family feuds, and, in general, fought external forces. In more sophisticated societies, new elements have altered the traditional ancient image of the hero. In the treat-

[1] Cesare Lombroso, with Rodolfo Laschi, *Il delitto politico e le rivulozioni* (Torino, 1890).

2

ment of historical events, men of the real world have been dressed in the garb of heroes. Not only have those who battled external powers been regarded as heroes but also, more and more, those who fought internal evils as well. An internal social change, a struggle for an enduring earthly value or a worthy cause within the hero's own domain, has replaced the spirited act in supernatural or superhuman realms, and so in the patterns of heroism the notable deeds against external forces have been increasingly expanded to include man's exploits in his own social surroundings.

These unmythical yet often legendary heroes—though part of history or sometimes even the makers of history—are in their characteristics and goals or aspirations reminiscent of what might be called political criminals. But in distinguishing political criminals from heroes, one may be tempted to see a remarkable paradox: The former failed while the latter succeeded in representing an accepted value or cause within their social group. Perhaps it is in this apparent absurdity that the real truth is to be found. To say that no history of any society can be traced without having political criminals recorded may not be too far from claiming that histories of societies cannot be faithfully and reliably told without registering the chronicles of failed heroes. Giambattista Vico's contention that man's nature is that of a historical being whose powers and capacities are subject to change [2] and J. G. von Herder's implication about the significance of viewing human actions and achievements in understanding history,[3] however discarded by some of the modern theorists,

---

[2] Giambattista Vico, *Scienza nuova* (1744).

[3] J. G. von Herder, *Ideen zur Philosophie der Geschichte der Menschheit* (1784–1791).

3

may support the seemingly inconsonant resemblance of the concept of heroes to the concept of political criminals.

There is no real need here, nor is there space, to offer the annals of those abundant and recurring historical events where political crimes and heroic stunts appear to comingle in a perplexing and puzzling picture so that the conceptual particles of the former are indistinguishable from those of the latter. It is still not quite clear, for example, whether the Athenians Harmodius and Aristogiton who in 514 B.C., assassinated Hipparchus, one of Pisistratus' sons, were politically alarmed murderers who simply intended to demonstrate their bitter stance against a tyranny by killing the oppressive ruler's child or whether they were social revolutionaries who could have become triumphant heroes if they had succeeded in mobilizing Greece and liberating the masses of ordinary men by their crime. Or, it is still open to argument whether Gaius Cassius Longinus, the moving spirit in the plot to murder Gaius Julius Caesar, and Marcus Junius Brutus, the symbolic embodiment of Roman republicanism, organized the conspiracy against the dictator to prevent him from being *rex* and reviving monarchy or if the striking of Caesar on the Ides of March in 44 B.C. was only the result of long-standing personal and political animosities. Was the Czech professor Jan Hus a martyr, tortured and burned at the stake in 1415 because he preached his vision of a simple and universal Christianity, or should his religious revolt be seen as a political crime against the ecclesiastical power that controlled the society? Were Count Lajos Batthyány and his thirteen senior officers heroes who fought for an independent Hungary, or were they executed in 1849 by order of the Austrian General Haynau because they contributed to the downfall of the Habsburgs and thus

4

committed some sort of treason? From the age of the Greeks and Romans or even earlier up to our time, it is indeed almost impossible to catalog all those whose political crime has been praised as heroism or whose heroic act remains degraded as a political offense.

If we look only at contemporary history, some of the most profound and in many instances irreversible changes are of the heroic or political varieties and are perhaps even more significant than concurrent scientific or technological innovations. The rise and fall of empires, charismatic leaders, races, classes, and social systems have been the dominating features of these changes, and almost without exception all changes paraded both heroes and political criminals. Moreover, perhaps stemming from the historically atypical rapidity and volume of these events, even within our own time many of those originally hailed as heroes have become political offenders and many of those regarded as political criminals have been elevated to the glorified pedestal of heroes. In our age the problem of political crime is more of a topical issue than it may have been in the past. But any analysis of our political criminals might be facilitated by the recognition that they do not really differ from those of bygone times. From the Greeks and Romans down to the present day most of them exhibit common elements. In fact, contemporary political criminals may generally be termed methodological kleptomaniacs who steal style from one another and from their historical "ancestors." Whereas the political criminals of antiquity may be characterized by commentators and writers as genuinely passionate offenders, those of our century are the same, but cloaked in modern technology.

If the problem of political crime is becoming more of a thematic issue than it was in earlier ages, and if we have difficulty feeling anything but disquiet at experiencing so many revolutions, upheavals, rebellions, and violent social movements, this is not because we resist a better future, but because there are so many various and confusing proposals for so many different, brilliant, and eloquently discrepant futures. And because of these violent political events, no one's life can remain untouched. While it is true that for centuries political crimes have often been the most powerful forces in shaping human societies, now we are living in an age in which the abuses of political criminality come more naturally to us than its uses, and the difficulty of distinguishing heroes from political offenders is increasing. It seems to me that Gustave Le Bon's vision of the leader manipulating the crowd was quite prophetic of the twentieth century. The popular use of the term "restructuring" has become mixed up with often empty-headed ideas of revolutionary alterations in society, which are sometimes rather far removed from a true concern for structuring. In our time the complaint that politics is being criminalized might be coupled with the complaint that criminality is being politicized. For those who believe that the world is, or should be, or tries to be a tolerant, humane, compassionate, and saintly honest universe, this is not the best of centuries.

While no era of history is without political crimes and heroic deeds, the real problem of the "modern" concept of the political criminal may be found in the fading out of the distinction between the "respectable" political criminals, or heroes, and the pseudoheroes and pseudopolitical criminals who have entered the arena where social changes for the benefit of people are being forced through violations of law. This is really where the concepts of justice, morality, and law appear to struggle the least with one another, and the comprehensible and gloomy realities emerge.

The Study of Crime Without Political Criminality

Although political crime is the oldest and perhaps most recurring criminal phenomenon of history, and because of its impact by all means the most important, it has been largely ignored in criminological studies and has been the subject of little research or analysis. It is almost as if it were considered a kind of criminological satellite, some strange body of law violation revolving around the concept of ordinary crimes. This neglect of political crime by criminology and the social sciences in general is all the more surprising because the available data are extensive and there are no peculiar difficulties in attempting to penetrate below their surface. It may be that the overly quantifying and behavioral approach of contemporary criminology and sociology (which tends to have only tenuous connection with depth and originality), combined with lack of interest in the philosophical bases of the crime problem, has made for more concern for the expressions and results of conduct than for the conduct itself.

Millions of words have been spoken and written about the crime problem, and it has been analyzed and dissected in all its different aspects. Yet it has not been recognized that the political crime is the crux of the problem. While political crime is not only ever-present but also becoming increasingly frequent and even fashionable, it is not seen as a dominant literary theme by criminologists and sociologists. Although the concepts of political crime and the political criminal are pivotal to the understanding of criminology, and maybe even truly critical to understanding law and the whole normative system of the society, political criminality seems to be the most undernourished area of sociology and contemporary criminology.

History demonstrates that there have been, and still are, plenty of times and places (one of them is believed to be the American society) where people become used to the threat of political violence as a normal part of daily life and where the theoretical treatment of political crime would thus appear to be of no practical value. But this is an astonishingly poor defense for the lack of literature on political crime, and the very silence itself may be a reinforcing factor for violent political acts. Although it is not out of place to think that few circumstances can be more embarrassing for a government than the discovery that an opposition is at work, suggestions that the major nations' reluctance to acknowledge criminal opposition, while viewing political offenders as insane or as ordinary lawbreakers without political beliefs, cannot be solidly substantiated. In any case, such suggestions would be poor excuses for the neglect of political criminality in the study of crime.

Even if this suspected aversion of the political power structure to admitting the reality of opposing political criminality were true, it could not apply to past history. The ancient Romans did not try to camouflage treacherous acts; they made a public spectacle of the punishment of traitors. The English, beginning with the laws of Alfred and Ethelred in the ninth century, have displayed a long list of sensational open trials of treason and sedition. And even in our century in the Soviet Union, at least under the reign of Joseph Dzhugashvili Stalin, the rulers have not been bashful in dealing with betrayals. On the contrary, they introduced morbid methods of persuasion to obtain confessions and to make political crimes more public and dramatic. Conversely, the report of the American National Commission on the Causes and Prevention of Violence in 1969 devoted several thousand printed pages to the many facets of violence, but despite the fact that the bulk of this report dealt with violent crimes clearly of a political character, the general problem of political crime and the concept of the political criminal were not discussed.

The relative nature of the political crime and the difficulties of defining it may be used as another excuse by the writers of sociological and criminological literature for their hesitant approaches to political criminality. Indeed, even in the field of interjurisdictional cooperation, where the problem of how to exempt political criminals from extradition often arises, international treaties usually avoid the concept of political crime. Wherever political crime is defined in agreements between sovereign powers, first perhaps in 1174 in the agreement between the English King Henry II and the Scottish King William the Lion, it is generally expressed in objective references to felonies committed against heads of state, treason, conspiracy, and mutiny. In the United States Thomas Jefferson, in 1792 as secretary of state in George Washington's administration, distinguished between ordinary criminals and those who are pursued by tyrannical laws, and thus left the definition of political crime open.

In 1854, a Jacquin attempted to assassinate Napoleon III by blowing up his train and afterwards escaped to Belgium. The Belgian government appeared to be hesitant in satisfying the French demand for extradition, and in

9

1856, in the famous "assassination clause," the Belgians added to their law of extradition and offered a negative definition of political crime by stating that an assassination attempt against the head of a foreign state is not a political crime if it consists of the elements of an ordinary homicide or poisoning.

The 1880 Oxford Congress of the Institute of International Law, in spite of its devotion to the problem of political crime, again reached an impasse by recommending a somewhat restricting definition confined to crimes committed in the course of insurrections and civil wars, but even in these cases only to those crimes which are otherwise "permissible" in a general war (*usages de la guerre*).

Many analysts of the issue of extradition see in the concept of political crime a characteristic offspring of the French terminology (*délit politique*), a kind of supralegal or metalegal category, which can be mirrored only in the interests of a given political power and, therefore, is beyond the descriptive ability of the law. Carrara, for example, labeled it simply "indefinable."[4] Others, however, who attempted to circumscribe what political crime means by approaching the concept from a variety of objective as well as subjective angles, have furnished the international law literature on extradition with hundreds of definitions, most of which are directed only toward serving interjurisdictional purposes.[5]

---

[4] Francesco Carrara, *Programma* (6th ed., Torino, 1886), para. 3916–3939.

[5] Objectivized definitions have been attempted by, among others, Bluntschli, Brusa, Carmignani, Crivellari, De Vigne, Fabreguettes, Finger, Fiore, Garraud, Gerland, Grivaz, Haus, Hélie, Holtzendorff, Homberger, Kleinschrod, Köhler, von Liszt, Löwenfeld, Martens, Martitz, Mecacci, Meyer-Allfeld, Mittermaier, Mohl,

Outside the sphere of international criminal law, particularly in sociological criminology, only a few scattered writers have regarded the political criminal as worthy of interest. Even these have seemed to confine themselves to the analysis of violence and other behavior patterns which usually accompany political crime. If political crime as a crime type is alluded to at all in some contemporary textbooks of sociology and criminology, it is treated only obliquely, although even definitional difficulties cannot excuse how the norm system, or crime in general, can be explained without involving the class of crime that contains all the basic problems of man's deviant or criminal conduct. In fact, the difficulties found in international criminal law in delimiting political crime and in qualifying the characteristics of the political criminal should have stimulated other fields of study and ought to serve as a guiding light in the bewildering labyrinthine world of the crime problem.

The uncertainty and vagueness which necessarily burden the concepts of political crime and the political criminal no doubt cloud the general understanding of the norms and especially the crime. Yet all crime theories, however sophisticated they try to be or might be, which neglect or ignore the puzzling questions raised by political criminality display varying degrees of theoretical astigmatism that may easily lead to almost total failure in interpreting the inevitable realities.

Ortolan, Pravo-Kluit, Prins, Rénault, Rossi, Schiattarella, Schirach, Teichmann, Transimeni, André Weiss. Subjectivized or motivational-type descriptions have been attempted by, among others, von Bar, Billot, Dalloz, Deloume, Georgi, Glaser, Lammasch, Soldan. Many are cited by George Rácz, *A politikai büntettesek menedékjogának kritikája* (Budapest, 1932), p. 25; and Ugo Conti, "Sul delitto politico," *Rivista penale*, vol. C., no. 1, p. 8.

The Significance of Political Criminality

Political crime is not only a historical and a contemporary phenomenon, but it is also surely one of the most popular myths of our time. It seems to be now widely understood and practiced in an allegorical sense by the masses in their quest for a better world. Its exquisite spiritual meaning is often expressed in vulgar political violence. All over the world, wrote the London *Times,* "men and women in search of hope cling to the belief that, in some sense, somehow, somewhere revolution will erupt to transform, permanently and beneficially, the present monstrous conditions of life." [6] But, the *Times* continues, the myth of revolution and political violence acts in some cases as a narcotic, freeing its victims from any felt need to grapple with actuality as they dream of the promised day. And, at the same time, it drives others to feverish actions which are often misguided, for they are oriented toward violence in order to achieve revolution that, again so often, turns out to be indifferent to immediate improvements in social conditions.

To be involved in political violence has been revealed not only as a kind of social medicine that offers momentary relief from the painful pressure of the world in our time, but also it has grown to be a modish behavior that is frequently confused with what political criminality really is. This is why violence tends to "help" only the individual participants. Today it is losing much of its sensationalism and ability to shock—although its victims are just as

[6] *The Times Literary Supplement,* no. 3,671, July 7, 1972, p. 763.

maimed or dead—because it has become so commonplace.

Many cultures have a vision of some ideal state of affairs, sometimes expressed in religious terms, at other times in secular ones—Valhalla, Nirvana, Paradise, or Classless Society. Our American visions of the future, however, seem to be less formulated. In many instances, we do not even have a clear vision and understanding of our present, except, and this cannot be denied, that we are bent under the heavy load of a great number and variety of social problems. Pascal Laine contended that the trouble with our society is the trouble of our time: This trouble is the *irrévolution*, that is, an overly generalized dissatisfaction, a criticism coming from so many with such destructive force that it may destroy us all.[7]

One may add to this cynical pessimism that this *irrévolution*, among other things, also indicates that only some, if any, of us may be termed "political criminals" in the true and historical sense. Many of us are just drifting toward what may be called political violence. However, the world of the real political criminal and his way of viewing society are convincingly different from those of persons involved only in violent political activities. This does not seem to be well understood by "the involved," and consequently their impressions and visions about the present and future of society often do not penetrate below the perception of the troublesome state of our world. It may be true that because of social changes and liberations from some strict underlying religious moral dogmas, society may not be built on, or may not function on, the bedrock of traditional Christianity any longer. But society is by no means a cesspool, as some of these drifting souls, whose critical ability sometimes narrows to the point

[7] Pascal Laine, *L'irrévolution* (Paris, 1971).

where undeniable realities are ignored, would have us believe.

Our turbulent world in this last lap of the twentieth century, with its abundance of recognized and torturing social problems, with its confusions, lack of goals, and aspiration-limiting, realistic societal roles, gives the impression that indeed our trouble is that we do not really know what our trouble is. So many people are demanding social change; others, at the same time, grumble about the pace of change, the decay of traditions, the size of cities, and the death of God. For two thousand years, for example, Jesus Christ has been just a humble messiah; but now "Jesus Christ Superstar" has opened on Broadway, with protesting picket lines of those who still believe in Jesus as the Savior rather than as a "showbiz" commodity on the one hand, and on the other hand with more tickets presold than for any other musical in theatrical history. The ordinary man of our world seems to be confused about himself as well as about others and the world in which he is expected to live.

Although men and women everywhere desperately hope for and demand social change, most of them cannot formulate their hopes or define the future they demand and they do not realize that sincerity and goodwill are not enough to remake the world. They cry out for change, but what exactly social change or "progress" means, they don't know—it is a puzzling Sirens' song that leads them on. There is indeed a fundamental and growing divergence in sociological opinion with regard to what social change is all about and what kind of social change could make man happy and content. Even among the true and devoted Marxists, American as well as East European, an opposition within has emerged, and it struggles for another Marxism that is even more difficult to reach than the one guided by the orthodox dogmas. In revisiting Marxism, it is no longer clear where to locate Karl Marx.

Granted that much is wrong with all known ideologies, the ordinary drifting man does not seem to be concerned with analyzing them. Under the pressure of his truly felt yet generalized discontent he is ready to accept any belief and to join any pseudopolitical criminal. He may even join the genuine political criminal who, by the way, is usually not simply an alienated individual who preaches and promises social change, but a solitary thinker and doer, most often expressing his case with decorum and deliberation.

The political criminal needs the support of the masses but is usually isolated from his followers, who try to achieve something that they think he is advocating. Those, and there are many, who find society as externally experienced an irritating fact, are easily "involved" in what they believe is the political criminal's cause, regardless of whether they understand him correctly or not. History, however, proves that even among the real political criminals only a very few achieve the monumental climax of their efforts. But the followers, those who are just involved, do not fall into the category of political criminals, and their usual unfortunate fate is to disappear. For these "involved" self-proclaimed heroes, involvement in political criminality almost always means just the performance of violence, and they end up in self-destruction, or at best in embittered, frustrated, and unsatisfied withdrawal. Their destiny is far from becoming *the* political criminals; they end by becoming political casualties.

Often, justified discontent is the seed, but learning is the process, that makes men become participants in the allegorical political violence that has grown from the myth of political crime and has now become a fashion or fad.

Its development is consonant with Gabriel Tarde's "laws of imitation" [8] or, in its modern version, with Edwin H. Sutherland's "differential association." [9] It is seen as a socially acquired behavior, learned through the processes of interpersonal relationships. The individual's confused personal identity, or his roleless self-concept, and the common core of disturbing social conditions are the bases of his involvement.[10] His participation in so-called political violence is encouraged by the fashionable current. Tarde explained this process by pointing out that man tends to imitate: The more contact among people the more imitation takes place, and a superior is usually imitated by his inferior. The genesis and growth of political violence in our time, in a variety of forms, proves Tarde's thesis.

Usually "the involved" is not "the thinker" or "the planner"; he only follows the catchwords and becomes entangled in sociopolitical issues that appeal to him emotionally. He then decides—often without understanding the realities—what the key is to the given social situation, he formulates it, and then he describes the situation in such a way as to prove to himself that he is right in his pseudoheroic violent act. Actually he is an innocent in political crime—he is just a victim of the spread of patterns of modish behavior. Certainly he is not a political criminal. The blame falls on the conditions of the world and on his making himself available to the fashionable current.

This is not to devalue the societal role the involved

[8] Gabriel Tarde, *La criminalité comparée* (Paris, 1890) and *La Philosophie pénale* (Paris, 1890).

[9] Edwin H. Sutherland, *Principles of Criminology* (3d ed., Chicago, 1939).

[10] See Stephen Schafer, *Theories in Criminology: Past and Present Philosophies of the Crime Problem* (New York, 1969), pp. 239ff.

plays in the awareness, the recognition, and even the appeasement of our burning and overwhelming social problems. To view his act as negligible or unimportant would depreciate and deflate the remarkable significance of the societal role of the masses. This is only to distinguish "the involved" from "the political criminal." They are in totally different categories. While the political criminal has the virtue of trying to expand the limits of the known, the involved is usually unable to reach even the known limits.

The significant concept of the political criminal necessary to an understanding of the general crime problem must not be confused with the concept of the involved discontented lawbreaker. The involved has no heroic elements and does not contribute to the understanding of the political criminal. These are two fundamentally and conceptually disparate and mismatched categories. Only a study of the true political criminal will shed light on the universal crime problem. The increased rate of political crime in the twentieth century should not be muddled with the fashionable involvement in political violence. When a better understanding of the concept of crime is attempted, only the concept of the true political criminal may help this effort.

2

The Relativity
of Political Crimes

Distinction Between Ordinary and Political Crimes

In the broadest sense, it may be argued that all crimes are political crimes inasmuch as all prohibitions with penal sanctions represent the defense of a given value system, or morality, in which the prevailing social power believes. Taking this to the very extreme, even a bank robbery, a shoplifting, or a rape is a political crime. After all, making such acts criminal offenses is a protection of the interests, values, and beliefs of the lawmaking power, actually the political-social system, which regards certain things as right and worthy of safeguarding with the threat of penal consequences.[1]

---

[1] A somewhat similar stand was taken by Maurice Parmelee in *Criminology* (New York, 1918), p. 92. Thorsten Sellin's "culture conflict" theory in *Culture Conflict and Crime* (Social Science Research Council, New York, 1938) may also not be far from supporting such a contention. The Soviet concept of "social danger" strongly leans toward such an understanding.

Whatever is called crime in law, by definition, constitutes a legal relationship between the official state and the members of the society. But this seemingly administrative and formalistic legal relationship is in its real essence a political relationship, since it pertains to the terms of existence between the state, as a political power, and the members of the society who live under this power, or rather, to the place and role of these men in their state. That is, it defines what is permitted and what is prohibited them in their political society. Thus, the legal relationship between the state and its members is an ideological-societal relationship where the stipulations of criminal law serve as safeguards of the various values of the ideology that the state power wants to see implemented. While it is not uncommon to meet arguments which strive admirably to propose that the political state power is for creating conditions to implement the values and goals of the society, the brutal reality suggests that the power creates the societal values and goals and enforces the conditions in which they are fulfilled.

Human behaviors that are qualified as crimes by the law, therefore, represent counterideological-societal conditions declared as nondesirable by the social-political state power. The interests, values, and beliefs of this power, whatever its operational structure may be, are expressed through legal norms. Among these norms are the rules and definitions of criminal law which, in order to enable the state to exercise control over accentuated ideological issues, declare certain acts to be crimes. In the definition of crimes, then, the state power's political ideology is translated into legal terms. Bank robbery, shoplifting, and rape, to mention examples, are crimes because the political state power ideologically believes in protecting other people's money, in allowing honest customers to browse through displayed goods in stores, and in protecting the bodily or sexual integrity of females. From this point of view, David Riesman's question, "Who has the power?" [2] and the contention of C. Wright Mills that the power is in the hands of an exploitative elite [3] are irrelevant, since all types of social powers are political powers and all have some kind of ideology mirrored by the criminal law.

When the political state power expresses its ideology, or value system. through the regulations of the criminal code, it determines the "norms of action" (*norma agendi*) and, at the same time, authorizes the executive organs of the state to apply penal sanctions in order to enforce the observance of these norms or, in other words, the acceptance of the value system. The question of which specific values or interests are so protected is dependent upon the legislators. as the political agents of the state power who conceive and pass criminal laws.

Since the analysis of what political crime is requires a conceptual rather than a definitional approach,[4] the general notion of political offenses might reasonably be equated with the concept of ordinary crimes. Whether it be treason, murder, drug use, embezzlement, homosexuality, arson, or whatever, ultimately and in the final examination, each is determined to be a crime by the legislators' philosophical, ideological, and political postures that con-

---

[2] David Riesman, "Who Has the Power?" in Reinhard Bendix and Seymour M. Lipset (eds.), *Class, Status and Power* (New York, 1966).

[3] C. Wright Mills, *The Power Elite* (New York, 1956).

[4] William Thomas Mallison, "Political Crimes in International Law: Concepts and Consequences," *Newsletter* of the American Section of the Association Internationale de Droit Pénale, no. 9 (December 1971), Washington, D.C., p. 10.

struct in the form of law "the formal expression of the value system of the prevailing social power."[5] Assuming this is so, the distinction between ordinary and political crimes becomes difficult to determine since all crimes might be viewed from the concept of political orientation and as ideological in nature. Thus, all crimes may be qualified as political crimes.

As a matter of fact, the more pronounced the ideology of the political-social power, and the less possible the participation of ordinary men and social groups in the decision-making processes, then the easier it is to see that all crimes are of a political nature. In the heavily ideological political structure, the concept of criminal responsibility is spelled out more vividly, the ideological basis of all crime definitions is less concealed, and the suprauniversalistic interpretation of the crime problem is more openly admitted. In this suprauniversalistic understanding of crime, the political-social power emphasizes the political ideology so that it stands above not only individual interests, but also above the conventional group interests of the society (that is, the interests of the "universe").[6]

While in other types of political structures the ideological foundations of the so-called ordinary crimes are not so apparent, and these crimes are most often seen only as disturbances of legally protected individual interests, in the suprauniversalistically oriented societies criminal law offers direct protection and care not so much to individuals or groups, but outrightly to the ideas of the ideology itself.

The German *Täterstrafrecht* (criminal law as it in-

[5] Stephen Schafer, *Theories in Criminology: Past and Present Philosophies of the Crime Problem* (New York, 1969), p. 17.
[6] Stephen Schafer, *The Victim and His Criminal: A Study in Functional Responsibility* (New York, 1968), pp. 33–36.

volves the criminal) in the Third Reich, for example, tended to disregard the rigidly formalistic definition of crimes and to establish the degree of responsibility in accordance with the political personality of the criminal, even if he was the perpetrator of a traditionally "ordinary" crime. This proposition, to some extent, separated the criminal from his objective relation to his crime and victim and subjected his human conduct to a judgment directed by the supreme ideology. This approach attempted to find what was called the "normative type" of criminal, and the penal consequences of his responsibility would be decided by the deviation of his personality— and not his actions—from the ideologically saturated and politically interpreted norm. Capital punishment under this concept would not necessarily be inflicted on a person who actually committed a murder, but on any individual who, in view of his total personality, should be regarded as a "murderer type," regardless of whether he committed a homicide or not.

This concept ideologized the interpretation of all crimes so extensively that the criminal act and its legal definition were no more than aids to the political evaluation of crimes. It suggested that the *Volksanschauung* (public view) cannot be satisfied with a simple "symptom" (that is, the criminal offense), because the criminal is not always what one particular crime makes him appear to be. Eric Wolf claimed that "political liberalism and religious naturalism" are over, and therefore the "ethically indifferent positivistic individualism" should be replaced by "phenomenological personalism." [7] Wolf as well as

---

[7] Eric Wolf, *Vom Wesen des Täters* (Berlin, 1932); "Richtiges Recht im nationalsozialistischen Staat," *Freiburger Universitätsreden*, vol. 13 (1934).

Georg Dahm,[8] the pioneers of this normative typology, emphasized an ideological understanding of crime, in fact of all crimes, and proposed that the *Volksanschauung* should operate to control "disobedience and resistance" against the "national socialistic state."

In this kind of elastic concept, which so strongly disregards any distinction between ordinary and political crimes, not the personal drama of the criminal and his victim, but the drama of the offender and the ideology is of paramount importance, and all crimes are actually confused with political sins. In this suprauniversalistic concept of crime, the virtual absence of ordinary offenses has substituted for the personal victim the idea of a victimized ideology. The net result of this exaggeration by which all crimes are seen as having political origins is, necessarily, the suppression of legal arguments, and it may ultimately make the judicial agents of the political-social power the definers of what a crime actually is.

In a less overtaxed exposition, the Soviet Union may be seen as another example where all crimes are soaked in the substance of ideology, and unreservedly political motives are injected even into what are conventionally called ordinary criminal offenses. In social structures like that of the Soviet Union and other socialist countries, where the political and economic system holds a crucially significant position and where a determined move toward an ideological goal represents the social dynamics, the traditional understanding of crime could not provide satisfactory protection of the system and its future development. In a socialist-type social structure that is projected

---

[8] Georg Dahm, "Die Erneuerung der Ehrenstrafrecht," *Deutsche Juristenzeitung,* 1934, *Der Tätertyp im Strafrecht* (Leipzig, 1940).

toward future goals and developments, law has little to do with the protection of what is usually called civil rights. That is, law sets few limitations on the state power's freedom to intrude on the individual man.

Consequently, a broader and stronger concept of criminal responsibility has to be created, based on an ideological and political interpretation of all criminal offenses. "A program of action" in the Soviet Union is "expected to improve the economic and political status of both peasants and workmen"; [9] therefore the question of criminal responsibility and the evaluation of crime factors have to yield to the supremacy of the governing political philosophy. "Not merely the act," writes Harold J. Berman, "but the 'whole man' is tried; at the same time, his crime is considered in the context of the 'whole community.' " [10]

Since the social control exercised by the political power is based on ideology-directed social defense, the interpretation of crime, whatever the criminal offense may be, and the criminal's responsibility are necessarily politically subjective. All crimes are viewed from the angle of the ruling doctrines as designed by those in power, and all criminals are evaluated and judged according to the political-ideological value of their crime target. Therefore, as John N. Hazard put it, even the "court is an instrument of state policy and by no means impartial." [11]

In view of the utmost importance of defending the ruling ideology and so protecting the political system, the central issue of the conception of all crimes in the Soviet Union and other socialist countries is the idea of "social

[9] John N. Hazard, *The Soviet System of Government* (Chicago, 1964), p. 2.

[10] Harold J. Berman, *Justice in the U.S.S.R.* (rev. ed., New York, 1963), p. 257.

[11] Hazard, *op. cit.*, p. 168.

danger." Although this term has been widely used since the time of the pioneering Enrico Ferri, socialist criminology has changed its original meaning to serve ideological purposes. Since crimes are "actions of the people's enemies, foreign agents, and their accomplices, wreckers and saboteurs, spies and traitors, and manifest forms of the open battle waged by the capitalistic world" against the socialist societies,[12] "the consequence of a human action, and especially the socially dangerous consequence, occupies a central place in the system of Soviet criminal law."[13] Any crime is a "social danger," meaning that it exposes the political and economic institutions, as the representations of the ideology, to harm, risk, or peril. Logically enough, the criminal is viewed in the same context; according to M. D. Shargorodskii and N. A. Beliaev, guilt means a person's *otnoshenie:* his mental attitude toward his socially dangerous conduct.[14]

The notion of social danger is not only "the pivot around which the whole system of Soviet criminal law is constructed,"[15] but also a flexible idea that makes it possible to establish the social dangerousness even *ex nunc,* rather than *ex tunc,* that is, at the time the act is being judged, rather than at the time it took place. This is all the less surprising since the Soviet criminal law, as one of the state superstructures by which power is imposed on the members of the society and one of the crucial pro-

[12] V. D. Menshagin, A. A. Gertsenzon, M. M. Ishaiev, A. A. Piontovskii, and B. S. Utevskii, *Szovjet Büntetöjog,* Egyetemi Tankönyv, official edition of the university textbook of the Soviet criminal law, in Hungarian (Budapest, 1951), p. 247.

[13] F. J. Feldbrugge, *Soviet Criminal Law: General Part* (Leyden, 1964), p. 101.

[14] M. D. Shargorodskii and N. A. Beliaev (eds.), *Sovetskoe Ugolovnoe Pravo, Obshchaia Chast* (Moscow, 1960), p. 313.

[15] Feldbrugge, *op. cit.,* p. 169.

tectors of the ruling power's ideology, has to approximate the political developments in the Soviet society, and the Soviet outlook on crime at any given moment has to reflect the changes, goals, and political decisions set by the authorities of the power.

The creators of the Napoleonic Code thought that they had prepared a legal system that would last for centuries, and they were not wholly wrong. Socialist lawmakers can have no similar long-range goals; inevitable developmental forces of the socialist system prevent making laws for generations or even for a decade or a year. This in itself explains why in the Soviet-type systems political thought dominates the concept of all crimes and makes the distinction between ordinary and political crimes obscure, if not in fact, absent. Or, viewed from the angle of the demands of the political ideological structure of this kind of society, it explains why traditional "guilt" has given way to the idea of social danger—danger to the political power's value system.

Nevertheless, even in those social systems where the political ideology of the ruling power is not so visibly involved in the understanding of crime and where the values of the political power do not strike the eye in reading the definitions of criminal offenses, the commonly believed distinction between ordinary and political crimes seems to come from a failure to consider the true profile of lawmaking.

The stiff qualitative separation of ordinary and political crimes can be seen as diametrically opposed to the real purpose of criminal law, actually the most important instrument of social control, which cannot tolerate ontological arguments in distinguishing between one crime and another by sorting them out into different classes. As a matter of fact, all crimes are socially dangerous, and all crime definitions reflect the value system of the social controllers. All social systems design one or another kind of social order, and all construct norms and rules to ensure the effective operation of the particular society. The violation of any of these norms and rules, to one degree or another, endangers the smooth operation of the particular political order. When Martitz claimed that the term "political crime" is an expression of the political language, and not the language of the law,[16] he did not pay attention to the real world's cruel fact that the language of the law in truth is the political language.

Indeed, criminal laws do not even distinguish between ordinary and political crimes, criminal codes just talk about crimes in general, even if the definition of one or another crime indicates the element of "political" motives, and only a few codes, if any, qualify certain criminal offenses explicitly as political crimes. The term "political crime," as commonly used, is not the offspring of criminal law. It is in fact a somewhat artificial and arbitrary product of international law which facilitates the processes of extradition and the possibility of offering asylum for certain fugitive criminals. How much of these crimes, then, demonstrates political motivation, and how much displays the components of a so-called ordinary crime, is a question that does not clearly lead to a general classification that would distinctly differentiate between the ordinary and political violations of law. The catalog of political crimes only shows that hardly any of them lack at least a portion of the act that would be judged as an ordinary criminal offense if they were not committed from political motives. This dioecious nature of political crimes

[16] Fr. Martitz, *Internationale Rechtschilfe in Strafsachen* (Leipzig, 1888/1897), vol. 1, p. 139.

prompted Heinrich Lammasch to call them relative offenses.[17]

However, in view of the political-ideological cradle of all crimes, it might be more appropriate to see the common or ordinary offenses as relative political crimes, as opposed to the absolute political crimes where the target of the lawbreaking is the ruling power's value system as a whole, rather than a part or an issue of it. Shoplifting and robbery, for example, are criminal attacks against the value attached to private property, and even abortion and homosexuality are assaults only against single issues of the political power's ideology. The political nature of these kinds of crimes is only occasionally conspicuous; thus, these "ordinary" crimes may be tentatively called "relative political crimes." But where the unlawful battery of the criminal is aimed at the sum total of the lawfully prevailing ideology or value system, or at least at one of its representative or critical institutions, for the sake of approaching the concept of the political criminal, and through that the problem of morality and crime, the violation of the legal norm might be called an "absolute political crime."

Lawmaking and Justice

The absolute political criminals, that is, those who inflict a criminal blow upon the ideology as a whole or who at least attempt to assault it, almost always act in the name of what they think is justice. They believe in an

---

[17] Heinrich Lammasch, *Das Recht der Auslieferung wegen politscher Verbrechen* (Vienna, 1884); *Auslieferungspflicht und Asylrecht* (Leipzig, 1887).

ideal universal concept of justice, often confused with morality, that would symbolize an unqualified, unconditional, and self-existent fairness, as they conceive it, and they usually refuse to accept the thesis which suggests that justice means only what those who are in power agree to make it mean.[18] They believe in the unjust nature of the prevailing value system and the law that reflects it, and they tend to reject hearing Northrop's question: Is there any objectively determinable standard, in other words an "is" other than the living law against which the goodness or badness of the living law can be measured? [19]

The political criminal is both appalled and perturbed by the a priorism, subjectivism, and complacency of the lawmakers, with their enthusiasm for sitting in armchairs and laying down the social-political power's law about the functioning of the human mind, the human predicament, and so forth, and their rationales for doing so. However, hardly any political criminal can be persuaded to assume that he himself would not act otherwise, should he be the one who is sitting in this armchair in the event that his crime, aimed at replacing other people's justice with his own, is successful.

The discrepancy between the ruling power and the political criminal on the nature of lawmaking and justice is a disconcerting theme common to all ages. The quest for an answer (incidentally, often neglected by sociological criminology in the search for social crime factors) has failed to achieve a comforting resolution. It offers only a frustrating and depressing experience to both parties as well as to those students of sociology and criminology who

[18] Schafer, *Theories*, p. xi.
[19] Filmer Stuart Cuckow Northrop, "Ethical Relativism in the Light of Recent Legal Science," *Journal of Philosophy*, vol. 51 (Nov. 10, 1955), pp. 649–662.

are interested in the puzzle of lawmaking and justice, or better, in the justice of lawmaking.

Law, in view of its representing the governing value system, is a political phenomenon. And, perhaps, the depth of this petulant disagreement on the meaning of the battered idea of justice between the ruling power and the absolute political criminal calls for the challenge of the tempering assumption that the two positions are logically not incompatible, appearances notwithstanding, since no lawmaking is really conceivable without manipulated justice. It is a familiar ground to students of the sociology of law that although the procedure of a trial, so the myth runs, is designed by neutral rules to find the truth, the judges are likely to confuse the combat against crime, which is their business, and the fight against broader social menace, which is not. The courtroom is almost always stuffed with the ruling power's value system, and the outcome of a case is dependent on the judges' perception of these values.

The painful pivot of the question to keep in mind is that both the bearer of the social-political power and the political criminal are men. Therefore, the man-committed crimes in general, and naturally among them the so-called political crimes, are dependent upon the man-made law, and, thus, as long as the existing power prevails, its understanding of justice, as ritually declared, is "right" and consequently must not be attacked beyond certain limits.[20] Since by definition the "conservatives" tend to conserve this justice, the "radicals" are those who attempt to change it, and thus are usually, or rather necessarily, the political criminals.

This idea probably motivated Havelock Ellis to sug-

---

[20] Schafer, *Theories, op. cit.,* p. 14.

gest that the word criminal in the expression "political criminal" is a euphemism to spell out the suppression of a small minority by the majority.[21] And while Hugo Grotius, from the opposite point of view, cited Tertullian, who proposed that every man is by birth a soldier with a mission to combat criminals guilty of treason, Louis Proal, a judge of the Court of Appeal at Aix, cited the anarchist Valliant, who proposed that the citizen has the same rights whether acting in self-defense against the tyrant or against an enemy.[22]

The question, of course, is who are the "radicals" and "anarchists" and who are the "conservatives," and which of them, and in what circumstances, are really the political criminals. The question inevitably leads to the problem of the relativity of law and justice, and, consequently, to the riddle of relativity in the concept of "absolute political crime," a characteristic that is only rarely obvious in the changing nature of "relative political crimes," or, as they are commonly called, "ordinary crimes." Ultimately it is a question that guides us to the understanding of man, should he be the powerful or the powerless—a multidimensional being whose consciousness, morality, justice, and freedom can be approached from different points of view, none of which can claim to be the only legitimate one.[23]

[21] Havelock Ellis, *The Criminal* (5th ed., New York, n.d.; preface to 4th ed., dated 1910), p. 2.

[22] Louis Proal, *Political Crime*, trans. unknown (New York, 1898), pp. 50–51, first published under the title *La criminalité politique* (Paris, 1895). To regard the state as criminal and the members of the society as victims is the crux of the problem and philosophically a highly controversial contention that leads to the problems of the natural law and to the assumption that there exists only a single justice.

[23] See Schafer, *Theories, op. cit.*, p. 11; also the general tone in Pratima Bowers, *Consciousness and Freedom* (London, 1971).

Perhaps this consideration led Havelock Ellis to contend that the word criminal in the term "political criminal" is "an abuse of language," and to suggest that such a concept may be necessary only to ensure the supremacy of a government, just as the concept of heresy is necessary to ensure the supremacy of the Church. The political criminal of our time or place, he argued, may be the hero, martyr, or saint of another age or land.[24] A monarch, for example, is the incarnate personification of conservation, and yet, as Maurice Parmelee contrasted, Charles I in England and Louis XVI in France were beheaded as political criminals. And, as he continued, altough "there is perhaps nothing in human culture more archaic than religion," under the French Revolution the clergy were proscribed as criminals.[25] To mention a more modern example, the abrupt and rapid changes in the lawmaking power structure at the time of the Hungarian revolution in 1956 resulted in criminals becoming heroes and then again criminals, and law-abiding citizens turning into criminals and then again into conformists—all within eight days.[26]

These few examples may sufficiently demonstrate that there is great complexity in the structure of the idea of justice and that the assessor of the battle between the lawmaking ruling power and the political criminal cannot safely determine which of them is supported by justice. The history of the philosophy of law, from the earliest beliefs in divine or superhuman commands to contemporary models of social engineering, could not reflect an agree-

---

[24] Ellis, *op. cit.*, pp. 1–2.
[25] Parmelee, *op. cit.*, p. 461.
[26] Stephen Schafer, "The Concept of the Political Criminal," *The Journal of Criminal Law, Criminology and Police Science,* vol. 62, no. 3 (1971), p. 381. Adapted by special permission.

ment in a universally valid formulation of what justice should really mean.

From the time of primitive societies, credulity regarding the supernatural has been present in one form or another, and much of the profound reverence for the gods is due to the deities having been garbed in the same sanctity as the human sovereign; the authority to decide the meaning of justice is also attributed to them. The great Christian philosophers of the Middle Ages turned away from the world around them to dream of a heavenly kingdom. The *City of God* of St. Augustine, the *Summa theologica* of Thomas Aquinas, and the works of others contended that justice is part of the law in the divine world, and man-made laws can reflect justice only if completely subordinated to God's order. Similarly, the idea of "earthly" justice, which emerged early in Greek philosophy, has also become a central target of speculative efforts. From the harsh and retributive Draconians through the Socratic-Platonic and Aristotelian views of natural law, the Epicureans' approach to justice oriented to human happiness, the Spinozian and Pufendorfian justice based on man's natural reason, to Kant's "categorical imperative," and many other thinkers' desperate and gloriously noble endeavors, an endless series of dignified mental struggles prove that the definition of an absolute justice or an unalterable and uniform law has not been found.

Even if the law could determine (as it cannot) "what resemblances and differences among individuals" are, to use H. L. A. Hart's words, and could recognize "if its rules are to treat like cases alike" in order to be regarded as "just," even if so, fundamental differences in political and moral views "may lead to irreconcilable differences and disagreement as to what characteristics of human beings are to be taken as relevant for the criticism of law as unjust." [27] Not even Hart's "minimum content of natural law," a strong hint that survival is a universal human goal [28] and an admirable struggle to save at least something for the "absolute" in lawmaking, seems to be able to avoid the emergence of what some people may regard as "injustice," since throughout the social history of man a great number of legal actions or laws have proved that the "justice of survival" has been justified with injustices.

This is not to eliminate the recognition of man's natural needs, a basic claim of the adherents of natural law who demand the consideration of some kind of inherent human rights in their attempt to construct the absolute justice. Neither Jeremy Bentham nor John Austin, to mention only two outstanding positivists, missed this consideration, although surely not to the satisfaction of our contemporary sociologists. Dennis Lloyd defends this stance by stating that it is not inconsistent with a positivist outlook to acknowledge the essential role of human values in law and society. "What the positivist rejects," he continues, "is neither valuations nor their effect on human institutions, but only the logical or practical possibility of establishing a scale of absolute values which govern mankind universally without distinction of time or place." [29]

When the political criminal assaults the ruling power's justice by claiming that it is unjust and by contending that his own justice is just, he might be right, but only in a relative sense. All laws are formulated on the un-

[27] Herbert Lionel Adolphus Hart, *The Concept of Law* (Oxford, 1961), p. 157.

[28] *Ibid.*, pp. 189–195.

[29] Dennis Lloyd, *Introduction to Jurisprudence*, with selected texts (2d ed., London, 1969), p. xvii.

spoken assumption that they are just and represent the right justice, even though they may not appear so to all members of the society and especially not to the political criminal. The laws are just and they reflect justice: This has to be learned by all aspirants of political crimes, at least insofar as they are defined by the ruling social-political power and so long as the existing power prevails. "For . . . what is Justice," suggested Thomas Hobbes in *Leviathan,* "there is need of the Ordinances of Sovereign Power." [30] This power, and not the political criminal, knows what is just or unjust, and in the form of commands or "ordinances" raises the law to the level of "justice." Cicero told the story of a captured pirate who defended himself before Alexander the Great by saying that he did exactly what the great conqueror did but that he was to be punished as a pirate rather than a conqueror just because he operated with a small boat rather than a large armada.[31]

Of course, the case of the pirate is not as simple as that. The question of who or what has the right to declare what right is, or who can claim his justice as just, is a centuries-old problem that has been studied by jurists as well as by sociologists. Perhaps one of the reasons for their long-standing disagreement in finding an answer is that lawyers are too close to the problem and sociologists are too distant from it, and both seem to be reluctant to meet in the domain of legal philosophy or in what is called the sociology of law. By the way, at this point it is difficult not to let slip the suggestion that one of the decisive factors in the impasse on the general crime problem is

[30] Thomas Hobbes, *Leviathan* (first publ. 1651), Part II, "Of Commonwealth," ch. XXVI, "Of Civill Lawes," p. 4.

[31] Cicero, *De republica,* III. 12.

our contemporary sociological criminologists' hesitancy to relate their etiological research to the speculations and findings of the philosophy of law and the norm system. Of course, much more is involved in the idea of law than sheer obedience and blind acceptance of the power-conceived justice and usually a rich and complex interplay among individuals, groups, and conflicting values takes place before a law is created. Yet, in the ultimate analysis, the definition and interpretation of justice, and lawmaking accordingly, are always monopolies in the exclusive possession and under the exclusive control of the social-political power.

The greatest obstacle to understanding this tenet is our reluctance to accept that what we think of as right and just does not necessarily represent the only correct view. We tend to think in terms of a single immutable truth and conclude that therefore there is only one possible system of justice. The claim that the social system and its law are just and fair rests upon the dubious hypothesis that there is only one just and fair code of values.

The political criminal gets involved in law violation by professing that his code is the only just and fair set of values, which represents the only justice. But the ruthless fact is that the social-political power has the monopolized authority to define justice. Exclusively this power defines the rightness or wrongness of the modes of human conduct. And whatever is defined by the ruling power as right or wrong, whatever is qualified as justice or injustice, must be accepted by those who are required to obey so long as the power is a "power." The relativity of the concept of the political criminal rests with this relativity of justice. In harmony with this precept one may argue for the assumption that all components of the problem of political criminality—law, justice, crime, power, and others—are relative and changing phenomena, and the ruling power is the central element that breeds this overall relativity.

The story of the "Lords Appellant," the plotters of the "loyal conspiracy" under Richard II in England, at the end of 1387, may serve as a historical example for demonstrating the crucial role of the political power's relative nature in generating the relativity of political crimes, and perhaps all crimes. The five magnates, Thomas of Woodstock the Duke of Gloucester, Richard the Earl of Arundel, Thomas the Earl of Warwick, Henry Bolingbroke the Earl of Derby, and Thomas Mowbray the Earl of Nottingham, revolted against Richard II. They wanted to make him their tool, and they named and "appealed" several of the King's close associates as traitors in the Parliament. However, a decade later Richard, having regained full power, took revenge by executing Arundel, murdering Gloucester, confiscating the lands of Warwick, and exiling Bolingbroke and Mowbray. Richard, who was only ten when he became king, after the reign of Edward III, inherited renewed outbreaks of political disorder, and he allegedly suffered a progressive mental disease that apparently helped to reduce his political commonsense and increase his somewhat fanatic and tyrannical manner of ruling. Yet he was the king: He made the law, distributed justice, and created the values, which had to be vacillating and changing. Anthony Goodman, who injected flesh and blood into theoretical analyses by examining this part of English history, contends that Richard II's reign was the crisis in a system of political conversions.[32] Indeed, the sovereign power shapes and molds the concept of justice

---

[32] Anthony Goodman, *The Loyal Conspiracy: The Lords Appellant under Richard II* (London, 1972).

in any given society, and it is this justice, changing even under the same reign, that may make the discontented man a political criminal and may lead him to act criminally for the sake of another justice he conceives.

The Sovereign's Command and the Dual Responsibility

To take a guided tour through the galleries of social-political power, including its intrinsic nature and societal process of development, is much too complex for such a brief treatise. But only the least sophisticated version need be understood to apply it to the problem of political criminality and to the crime problem in general. A mythological example may help to explain it: when Xerxes caned the furious waves for their disobedience, it could have been argued that the waves were responsible and that they should be punished for disobeying the Great King's order. But Xerxes should have been more concerned with the nature of their resistance.[33] Most criminological theorists, like Xerxes, try to explain criminal behavior itself, but they do not concern themselves with *why* certain acts are defined as crimes. The problem of crime, both political and so-called nonpolitical, consists of two interconnected elements: the acts defined in law as crimes and the forces that impel some people to commit these acts.[34] Both elements involve responsibility, but of two different kinds.

[33] See Schafer, *Theories, op. cit.*, pp. 6–14.
[34] The qualifying force of the law that judges a human behavior as criminal must not be confused with the sociologically popular "labeling" action coming from members of the society. While the former's source is the ruling social-political power, the

One kind is the responsibility of individuals who have acted in such a way that they are threatened with punishment under the law. Causing damage to anything pertaining to the military in time of war, with an intent to impair the war effort of one's country, can result in a person being held responsible for sabotage. Misappropriation or misapplication of money entrusted to a person's care may cause him to be held responsible for embezzlement. A person who willfully or maliciously sets fire to something, with or without intent to defraud, may be held responsible for arson. Anyone who steals, using force or violence, is charged with responsibility for robbery. These and other acts are imbued with responsibility by lawmakers who reflect the value system of the ruling power. Penal sanctions remain only abstract threats so long as the law is respected, or at least obeyed.

The second kind of responsibility concerns the forces that motivate someone to act against the law. What factors are "responsible" for a person becoming a saboteur, an embezzler, an arsonist, or a robber? Is it something in his biological makeup, in his psyche, or in his environment? Or does he "want" to act in a criminal way, and thus does he accept responsibility for his act?

Who can be made responsible and why? And what is responsible for making a person commit a criminal act? These are the two crucial issues, the understanding of

---

latter indicates an emotionally interwoven societal evaluation dangerously close to what is called public opinion. The "labeling theories," in sociology recognized as if they were new paths in understanding deviant behavior, actually deal with a centuries-old problem, more correctly called the "social consequences" of conviction or otherwise disapproved conduct. See, among others, Enrico Ferri, *La sociologia criminale* (Torino, 1884), art. 239.

which may lead to a better insight into political crime and therefore into crime in general. The answers to both questions will change as the values of the society change. So both responsibilities continually fluctuate.

Individual legal accountability or culpability for having engaged in punishable conduct should not be confused with the concept of responsibility as used here. "Answerability" is perhaps a more accurate term, for this responsibility includes the lawmaker's definition of crime and the individual's reaction to the law by breaking it—both are elements of a single continuum.[35] An intimate knowledge of the law and lawmaking is necessary for a complete understanding of criminal acts (this is what is not always well understood by sociologists). At the same time, criminal law cannot be fully comprehended without some understanding of the etiology of crime (this is what is not always well understood by lawyers). Without these two approaches to the understanding of the two responsibilities, crime may remain unknown.

The two responsibilities are interrelated and cannot be disconnected. This twofold concept seems to be the heart of the crime problem, regardless of whether one is

[35] H. L. A. Hart in his *Punishment and Responsibility* (Oxford, 1968), pp. 211–212, called attention to the wide range of ideas covered by the term "responsibility" in and out of the law. Hart distinguished among role responsibility, causal responsibility, liability responsibility, and capacity responsibility. In the present context, liability responsibility is the one charged by the lawmaking social-political power (it is role responsibility only in its moral sense as a general obligation of all members of the society), and causal responsibility would refer to the causes of crime or to its precipitating factors. Capacity responsibility, as concrete accountability, is merely a legal and often technical question beyond the scope of the present problem.

concerned with political crimes (absolute political crimes) or ordinary crimes (relative political crimes). The struggle between the threatening responsibility (mirroring the power's value system) and the counterresponsibility (reflecting the stand against the power) is dynamically ever-present. Without the former we would have a lawless and, consequently, a "crimeless" society; yet with it, we are unlikely to see crime disappear.

Changes in the law are not inevitably followed by changes in human conduct. A new law requires adjustment in individual behavior, but not all members of the society may so adjust, particularly if the new law involves prime political issues which touch upon the totality of the power's value system. Changes in law are variables that are almost never perfectly correlated with changes in society. Any number of contributory, contingent, and alternative conditions may strongly affect the relationship between law and criminal behavior. However, generally speaking, the criminal conduct will be the dependent variable. Man commits crime, but—and it cannot be repeated and emphasized enough—man makes the law that defines crime.

A system of absolute justice has yet to be invented, and so all lawmaking powers have invented their own unique systems of social control, which continually change. A constant and eternal "natural" law would be possible only if all social phenomena, and all lawmaking powers, were unchangingly uniform, or if all human beings at all times would agree to the validity of a single value system and all lawmaking powers at all times would unanimously support it. An accurate explanation of the causes of crime could be arrived at only if an immutable natural law existed. Raffaele Garofalo's analysis of "natural" crime, for example, is never ultimately convincing.[36] The "responsibility" for criminal conduct is so central to any criminological analysis that it is easy to neglect the crucial point—criminal law continually changes.

An individual's frame of reference, therefore, cannot be "naturally" consistent with his society's demands. He must adjust his conduct to the changes in the value system. Even if there appears to be a resemblance between the laws of two different control systems, interpretations and applications of the law invariably differ because the lawmaking powers use them differently. The concept of responsibility fluctuates bewilderingly from society to society and from one generation to the next. Man has always been aware of its inconsistencies, for it is this that makes the distinction between conformists and criminals. As Morris Cohen phrased it, "The legal system of any country has a definite history which helps us to understand its provisions and shows how it changes according to varying social conditions, and even according to the will of certain powerful individuals." [37]

Crime apparently does not change, but responsibility does. One person might go through life without ever being disturbed by significant changes of law, while another, in a different society, might be exposed to painful changes in the system of responsibilities, which require extreme changes in his behavior. Change in law is inherent in the law itself. It is possible to understand a system of law without understanding crime, but it is impossible to under-

---

[36] Raffaele Garofalo, *Criminology,* trans. Robert Wyness Millar (Boston, 1914).

[37] Morris Raphael Cohen, *Reason and Law* (New York, 1961), p. 12.

stand crime without understanding its relationship to the responsibility-making law.

The ruling social-political power is the source of responsibility-making law. Only support by the power makes it possible for a law to become "the law." Inversely, from the law we can discover its source: A particular concept of responsibility reflects the values of the lawmaking power. John Austin maintained that the law is the "command of the sovereign," [38] and Gustav Radbruch extended this statement by contending, in an explanatory fashion, that absolute justice is undiscoverable.[39] A combination of Austin's dictate with a Radbruchian relativism would imply that the lawmaking power may be acquired by any group or any individual at a given moment in time. E. Adamson Hoebel argues that Sir Henry Maine [40] was wrong in suggesting that early legal prohibitions seemed similar to a "despotic father's commands." [41] But Morris Cohen bluntly proclaimed the brutal truth: "Doubtless, the law will never, so long as it is administered by human beings, be free from arbitrary and brute force." [42]

[38] John Austin, *Lectures on Jurisprudence or the Philosophy of Positive Law* (London, 1861). Austin's first six lectures were published in his lifetime under the title *The Province of Jurisprudence Determined* (1832); the rest were published with the assistance of his widow.

[39] Gustav Radbruch, *Rechtsphilosophie* (3d ed., Berlin, 1932).

[40] Sir Henry Sumner Maine, *Ancient Law: Its Connection with the Early History of Society and Its Relation to Modern Ideas* (1861), with Introduction and Notes by Sir Frederick Pollock (London, 1906).

[41] E. Adamson Hoebel, *The Law of Primitive Man: A Study in Comparative Legal Dynamics* (Cambridge, Mass., 1954), pp. 258–259.

[42] Cohen, *op. cit.*, p. 112.

44

Hägerström,[43] followed by Olivecrona,[44] Lundstedt,[45] Ross,[46] Castberg,[47] and others—the so-called "Scandinavian Realists"—tried to be less harsh. Ross refers to the commands of the sovereign as "directives," and Olivecrona describes them as "independent imperatives." But essentially they are only terminological variations of Austin's authoritative expression Whatever term is used, the implication is that the law cannot be implemented without the threat of punishment. The disagreement between the Austinian stand and Hans Kelsen's views,[48] which find coercion in this threat, is indeed irrelevant in regard to the powerfulness of the command, since it invokes only the procedural problems of threatening with punishment and how to carry out the threats, if it comes to that.

Desire and fear are the two chief motivations for human behavior, no matter what sophisticated language we may use to say this in order to appear humane or civilized. It is by manipulation of these motivations that power maintains itself. Power without authority is meaningless, and authority is created by the people's belief that the holder of the power knows what they need and will satisfy that need, even if it must use force against those who do not understand what the need is. Max Weber, in discussing

[43] Axel Anders Theodor Hagerström, *Inquiries into the Nature of Law and Morals*, trans. C. D. Broad (Uppsala, 1953).

[44] Knut Hans Karl Olivecrona, *Law as Fact*, trans. unknown (Copenhagen and London, 1939).

[45] Anders Vilhelm Lundstedt, *Legal Thinking Revised: My Own Views on Law*, trans. unknown (Stockholm, 1956).

[46] Alf Ross, *On Law and Justice*, trans. Margaret Dutton (London, 1958).

[47] Frede Castberg, *Problems of Legal Philosophy*, trans. unknown (Oslo, 1957)

[48] Hans Kelsen, *Allgemeine Staatslehre* (Berlin, 1925).

45

power and legitimacy, doubted that the "absurd" would arise in practice,[49] but he lived before the many political crimes and revolutonary changes of the last half century, when throughout the world traditions and old truths have been demolished and new truths proclaimed, often by force. The man who experiences the truths of the ruling social-political power, whatever beliefs he himself has, appears to be held at gunpoint by the values of the power structure.

Lon Fuller, in his somewhat naturalistic search for "justice" in law, maintained that "there is no doubt that a legal system derives its ultimate support from a sense of being 'right.'"[50] But Edward Westermarck, who analyzed the development of moral ideas, concludes that, irrespective of the "sense" of right or wrong, the "law expresses a rule of duty by making an act or omission which is regarded as wrong a crime."[51] Dennis Lloyd proposed that the man who demands the obedience of others should be entitled to it.[52] But in the confrontation between the ruling power and the political criminal, the legitimacy of the power is often based on the power of the power. Maybe Hart was closer to the truth when he proposed that a penal statute declaring certain conduct as criminal and specifying the punishment to which the criminal is liable "may appear to be the gunman situation writ large."[53] Admittedly the lawmaking power cannot be identified with a

[49] Max Weber, *Grundriss der Sozialökonomie, III, Abteilung, Wirtschaft und Gesellschaft* (Tübingen, 1922), p. 28 and *passim*.

[50] Lon L. Fuller, *The Morality of Law* (New Haven, Conn., and London, 1964), p. 138.

[51] Edward Westermarck, *The Origin and Development of the Moral Ideas* (2d ed., London, 1912), vol. 1, p. 168.

[52] Dennis Lloyd, *The Idea of Law* (Baltimore, 1964), pp. 27–28.

[53] Hart, *Concept of Law, op. cit.*, pp. 6–7.

gunman simply because it has the coercive force to make others obey its commands, but there are intrinsic similarities between the two situations. For example, the death penalty and first degree murder differ only in their legality, as determined by conventional society.

Although from the Justinian Law to our own time, many value systems and laws have been born in dictatorial situations, the gunman circumstances are not really typical of the responsibility-making processes. Timasheff said, "A law of revolutionary origin may exist as well as a law of traditional origin," [54] but this is just a procedural issue. Austin's claim that in the last analysis the law is the command of the sovereign may be a gloomy truth, whether the origin of law is traditional or revolutionary. Franz Neumann, in his discussion of the terror of the Nazi regime, is right in maintaining that "the average lawyer will be repelled by the idea that there can be a legal system that is nothing more than a means of terrorizing people"; but this holds true only in practical terms, not in theory. The very fact that this unforgettable terrorism happened in a largely legalized fashion and resulted in lawful massacre, without parallel in history, justifies the theory.[55] Austin may have oversimplified the essence of lawmaking, but in the real world his tenet seems uncomfortably correct.

In the idea of law "the factor of obedience is . . . a crucial one," [56] Lloyd maintained, although he agreed that much more was involved. Who has the sovereign power, what legalities or formalities must be observed,

[54] Nicholas S. Timasheff, *An Introduction to the Sociology of Law* (Cambridge, Mass., 1939), p. 214.

[55] Franz Neumann, *Behemoth: The Structure and Practice of National Socialism, 1933–1944* (New York, 1963), p. 440.

[56] Lloyd, *The Idea of Law, op. cit.,* p. 27.

and what behavior or constitutional administration is required—these questions do not affect the fundamental structure of lawmaking. If the state were equated with the social-political power, Hans Kelsen's theory on the identity of state and law [57] would be closer to John Austin's position.

A single man, such as a despotic dictator, or many men, such as a democratic parliament, may be the lawmaking power. As Mannheim said, "The source of authority may be . . . the words of a prophet or a saint." [58] But the power makes the laws and defines responsibility, and as transfers in power occur, the laws and definitions change. Because there is discontinuity in the source of law, it is difficult to hold to an idea of continuity of law. The inevitable changes of the participants in the lawmaking process alone account for unavoidable changes in the definition of crime.

In all societies absolute political criminals may appear to be alike because they assault the value system of the ruling social-political power, but because the values vary, the political criminals in one society may really be very different from those in another. *Lex posterior derogat priori:* The law of yesterday may not be the law of today if it is no longer supported by the ultimate power in the society. The current law and the current value system supersede earlier ones. In some societies the legal code appears to be extremely stable, with only minor changes, but this "continuity" of the law is proved a fiction when examined closely. It is impossible to speak about "causes" of crime or crime "in general" without an awareness of the

[57] Kelsen, *op. cit.*

[58] Karl Mannheim, *Systematic Sociology: An Introduction to the Study of Society,* J. S. Erös and W. A. C. Stewart (eds.) (New York, 1957), p. 126.

forces that create and enforce the law and the manner in which the forces themselves change, and here lies the weakness of much contemporary criminological research.

Whether a man is a criminal or not depends on how he responds to the system of control in his society, as it has been introduced by the given ruling power whose aim is to establish or fortify its own ideal social order. A balanced assessment of political crime, or any criminal behavior, can only be achieved by studying the problem relative to the changing law. The relationship and correlation between legal prohibition and criminal action are much too intricate to be measured by conventional methods. The observer's own frame of reference becomes a factor in any judgment. The correlation between making people responsible for engaging in crime and the factors that produce noncompliance largely determine the relative significance of all crimes and the success of the power-designed social order.

The Changing Concept of Guilt of the Political Criminal

"All reputations, except those of the utterly imbecile, dwindle and rise again; capable men are praised twice, first for the wrong reasons and then after a cycle of obloquy, for the right." Chesterton wrote this sentence in defense of Macaulay, and it is close enough to describe not only some authors or scholars, but also the careers of some political criminals, although certainly not all. But the changing concept of political crime and the relativity of law, however true they are, are not adequate defenses and cannot secure asylum for all those who take a law-violating stand against the prevailing social-political power and its value system. The judgment of history may change their guilt to innocence and approve their act at some posttrial time, but only, as shown by the records, for exceptional political criminals. While the guilt of the political criminal is most often established immediately at the time of the act by the courts of justice, his innocence or his acquittal may be determined by the writers of history sometimes even centuries later. To be elevated to sainthood takes time.

However, the hundred years required to see a candidate successfully through to sainthood can exhaust the time and money of the sponsors, and the political criminal's own generation often witnesses only an abortive proposal of a changed verdict and can see him only as a guilty man. Before the cosmetic of political history labels his defeat as unjust, if it does so at all, he is unavoidably subject to the Austinian "command of the sovereign." Rarely does a person become a legend in his own lifetime. Saint Joan of Arc, the Maid of Orleans, the peasant girl who, acting as she believed under divine inspiration, led the French to a victory and Charles VII to his coronation at Reims, was soon afterwards captured and burned. Her postmortem rehabilitation did not change the fact of her execution, and she was not canonized by Pope Benedict XV until five hundred years afterwards—and even then not for her patriotism, but for the virtue of her life and her faithfulness to God.

Although recorders of historical facts have been interested in man's political behavior since the time of Herodotus and Thucydides, none of them could change the record for the political criminal who stood up against the sovereign and came to a fatal end. The command of the sovereign might later be seen as mistaken or wrong by historians, but at the time it was issued it was, by definition, necessarily correct and right. In view of the relativity of crime and the changing nature of law, the guilt of the political criminal may change *in thesi,* but it does not in fact. The political criminal's hope for vindication in eternity, even if justified, would hardly change the sovereign's belief that the offender must be disgraced by deterrent punishment, and no member of the society under the sovereign's rule will be allowed to see the offender other than as a criminal.

Actually, both the sovereign and his opponent, the political criminal, seem to be convinced that they are clear-sighted about the durability of their values, and both are confident of the favorable judgment of history. But they tend to overlook the fact that mythology grows slowly, and it may cause pain hundreds of years later. In our century, when the number of political criminals is increasing shockingly, more and more writers, speakers, and politicians believe and tell us that the offenders are foreseeing the future, but at the same time, more and more reports suggest that they are wrong. Quite often many of those personally familiar with an event that is destined to become historical, and from which they draw conclusions about the future, have difficulty remembering correctly what the event really was like. This is why writers of history are important people: One lifetime is not long enough both for the facts and the truth.

History is not only a myth-maker, it is myth-breaker too. As a result, in attempting to explain the structure of political crime in general, in spite of the abundance of research material, the social scientist is at a peculiar disadvantage. Unlike his colleagues who are investigating other social phenomena and unlike other scientists, he is unable to subject his specimens to laboratory tests. He has to rely on the writers of history, and although "history repeats itself," all he can do is to form a historically supported imaginary model.

It is often assumed that a man is better understood by posterity than by his contemporaries, and therefore that posterity can better judge whether the ruling social-political power was "right" or "wrong" in qualifying its opponent as a political criminal. If to be a man born out of one's time means no more than being neglected or even persecuted in one's own day and famous later, then the cliché does not misrepresent the facts. If so, reading history is good medicine against despair. However, this is not always the case, and the unpredictable future writers of history may not make heroes of all political criminals. Moreover, they may dress up heroes with criminal characteristics. No one can safely forecast how the political criminal's guilt will "change," if it changes at all.

That the political criminal is guilty at the time of his act against the sovereign power is beyond question. The puzzle of the changing concept of his guilt, however, lies with the value system of the history writer or even with the kind of values the ruling social-political power represents under which the writer of history writes the history of the political criminal's guilt. No one would deny that history, as written, is only a partial view of reality: How can a historian fail to reflect his own values and the values of his world? No master of the historical microscope, even if applying his instrument with rigorous care to past events, can see history without involving his own and his society's value system.

"History" consists of stories which may even be invented about the past; this is done just to define our relation to that past, or more simply to define ourselves. As Eugene Waith contended, the heroic is actually not a kind of person or action, but a way of looking at persons and actions.[59] In a similar vein it can be seen that the guilt of the political criminal, as judged from a historical distance, is not necessarily the actor's legally established culpability for a specified criminal offense. Rather it is his "sinfulness" according to the values and political outlook of the writer of his history. The moral to be drawn from the stories of political criminals is wholly dependent upon the general sociopolitical value stance of the man who undertakes the job of passing a sentence over the sentence passed by the court of justice.

The assessment of the relativity of historical judgments is no more pertinent to the understanding of political criminality than are the relativity of the ruling power and its law and the relativity of the concept of political crime itself. When attempting to evaluate and define the guilt or innocence and the greatness or insignificance of political criminals in historical perspectives, one has to stand, like a fashionable portrait painter, at a respectful distance. The way the model is seen is unavoidably affected by the specific personal or contemporary values of the viewer and often influenced by his emotions. The painter may be sympathetic if slightly quizzical, or he may be antagonistic, or neither. The result may be a polished portrait, glossy and refined; it may be illusion or reality; perhaps it may be too highly polished to reveal the magnanimity of the portrayed political criminal or too crude to show what a humbug the sitter really was.

Some writers of history try to devaluate important individuals by enhancing their guilt or by leaving their guilt as political criminals unquestioned, as it was at the time of their conviction. Others try to rescue insignificant persons from oblivion, or by "acquitting" the guilty ones

[59] Eugene M. Waith, *Ideas of Greatness* (London, 1971).

they try to resurrect them to the world of innocence or even praise. History can not only kill those who may deserve immortality, but also it can create memorable characters who appear credible.

History is not only unpredictable, but, in view of its necessary relativity, it is not, and it cannot be, an objectively safe compass. Yet the possible deflection of its magnetic needle is still not so misleading as the immediate vision of immediate events often is, and it offers the only chance to the political criminal, found guilty in his own time, to have his guilt made relative. As time wears on, the opportunity to see the political offender's criminality differently, as either better or worse, becomes more and more likely.

It is indeed unfortunate that the history of the recent past and even the history of the present have characteristics which set them apart from earlier periods. Today we seem to be too impatient to wait for chronological ripeness, and in our time we tend to write the history of our time. One of the merits of today's overeager historians is that they record the evidence on the basis of which the portrait of a political criminal could be reconstructed later; their demerit is that in spite of having the evidence, they themselves fail to reconstruct. Thus the value of the instructive relativity of the political criminal's guilt is weakened, since it may not be approached through the comparative assessment of different value systems. The distance between the political criminal's legally established guilt and its later reevaluation appears to be shrinking. While history may now be written by those who have not lived through, at least not in their maturity, the time of their subject matter, it can be read by those who have. These writers, then, may easily be caught out in errors by their elders who recollect what actually happened.

Hastily written immediate histories of political criminals are a risky business. While they can tell the true facts, they do not have the benefit of distance, or of the global truth that comes not only from the experience of those who lived through the event but also from writers of a period just before the given political crime. More often than not such histories seem to be more merciful and forgiving judges than the professional lawyers who actually convicted the political criminal. In the writings of history, political criminals of centuries ago have usually a more difficult case than those in the recent past. While only exceptional offenders of the distant past have received clearance from posterity, many more who have been found guilty in our century have succeeded in raising doubts about the justification for their convictions. History can never be an infallible judge of the political criminal's judges, yet the distance separating the historical judge from the crime creates a value universe that, dependent upon the size of this universe, can increase or reduce the degree of bias or prejudice of the judgment.

3

Morality and Political Crime

The Problem of Morality and Criminal Law

The two formidable concepts, morality and criminal law, stand in mutual relationship; both are heavily charged with apparently insoluble problems, even when treated independently of each other.[1] Lon Fuller found the literature on law and morality "deficient,"[2] and even Jeremy Bentham and Rudolf Ihering, who spent their lives studying these ideas, achieved only minimal success. H. L. A. Hart contended that they were perennial issues, and while he found many different kinds of relations between law and morality, he could not avoid discussing various aspects of these concepts also in terms of "jus-

[1] See Stephen Schafer, *Theories in Criminology: Past and Present Philosophies of the Crime Problem* (New York, 1969), pp. 62–91.
[2] Lon L. Fuller, *The Morality of Law* (New Haven, Conn., and London, 1964), p. 3.

57

tice." [3] Rusztem Vámbéry asserted that a full treatment of the subject would go beyond his capability just as it would be beyond the patience of the reader.[4]

However, no critical penetration into the political crime problem can be made without confronting the moral aspects which are at its center. The public does not necessarily see crime and immorality as synonymous. The relative and changing nature of the guilt of political criminals, especially, can be determined only by the history writers' support of the distinction between criminal law and morality, which makes morality often appear independent of the concept of justice and separate from law.

The claim for morality in the law has a base in man's earliest history. The Ten Commandments are not only an ethical code and a divine declaration, but they are also a body of criminal law norms. A. S. Diamond found several ancient codes free of religious dominance,[5] but Sir Henry Sumner Maine found that the origin of law was in religion.[6] Who was right is perhaps relevant only to their dispute about the relationship between religion and morality, which has nothing much to do with the discussion here. It is indisputable that religion and morality were allied in primitive societies, but we cannot determine the chronology and degree of their merger.

Even in our time there are strong indications of the continuing belief in God's role in designing and deciding

[3] Herbert Lionel Adolphus Hart, The Concept of Law (Oxford, 1961), p. 151 and passim.
[4] Rusztem Vámbéry, Büntetöjog és ethika (Budapest, 1907), p. 1.
[5] A. S. Diamond, Primitive Law (London, 1935).
[6] Sir Henry Sumner Maine, Ancient Law: Its Connection with the Early History of Society and Its Relation to Modern Ideas (1861), with Introduction and Notes by Sir Frederick Pollock (London, 1906).

morality, especially when so-called immoral acts are resented. As M. B. Ahern contended, given the existence of evil, credence in God can logically be maintained,[7] and it is a widely held sentimental belief that these two antitheses guide our moral stand. The spread of materialistic thinking and the obsession with technological advancements have not succeeded in making this engineer of good and morality dead. When God is unobtainable at his usual address, it is amazing what men will do to tempt Him back. Nicholas Timasheff's caution is well taken: "The question of the religious roots and interconnection of primitive ethics depends very much on what religion is considered to be and on what sort of connection is asserted."[8]

Edward Westermarck stated that "as men are concerned about the conduct of their fellow men towards their gods so gods are in many cases concerned about men's conduct towards one another, disapproving of vice and punishing the wicked, approving of virtue and rewarding the good"; but Westermarck knew this was not universal.[9] Although he listed a number of primitive peoples who believed in the existence of gods as the moral lawgivers or judges, he also gave examples of deities who were disinterested in the moral affairs of humans.

Crime, vice, and sin were indistinguishable in most primitive societies. Even today religion plays a major role in lawmaking if the social definition of wrongdoing in part determines the law and if, at the same time, the social definition of right and wrong stems from theological concepts. Consequently crime, vice, and sin may be viewed as

[7] M. B. Ahern, *The Problem of Evil* (London, 1971).

[8] Nicholas S. Timasheff, *An Introduction to the Sociology of Law* (Cambridge, Mass., 1939), pp. 275–276.

[9] Edward Westermarck, *The Origin and Development of the Moral Ideas* (2d ed., London, 1912), vol. 2, p. 663 and *passim*.

merged, and, at the same time, as functioning separately. In ancient Greece and Egypt, law, morals, and religion were integrated into a single idea, but in modern times man has become increasingly accustomed "to the purely secular conception of law as made by man for man and to be judged accordingly in purely human terms." [10]

Even an elementary acquaintance with criminal law makes it evident that many legal commands, past as well as present, are clearly formalized and legalized statements of religious doctrines. Homicide, theft, rape, perjury, and other offenses violate the code of law just as much as they run counter to ethical and religious strictures. All three codes actually regulate human behavior. The common origin of law, morality, and religion largely remains a mystery.

How much of criminal law was derived from ethical beliefs, and, particularly, how much of the judgments of political criminals are based on general moral views? Should moral factors influence the lawmaker? Can a criminal law oppose a moral command? Or, in other words, can a political criminal be legally wrong and morally right, or the reverse? Is a "just" criminal law's "morality" identical with its "justice"? What is the relationship between legal and moral obligations? How can one reconcile, if necessary and if possible, legal and moral responsibilities, and is it a necessary condition of social life that they should be in harmony? What is or should be the role of morality in preventing political offenses and crimes in general? All these questions are interconnected and are suggested by the relations between law and morality. Hart correctly proposed that there are so many different relations between the two that "there is nothing which can be

---

[10] Dennis Lloyd, *The Idea of Law* (Baltimore, 1964), p. 46.

profitably singled out for study as *the* relation between them." [11]

Bonds Between Morality and Natural Law

If morality is understood as some eternal and true justice created by a superhuman or immortal agency, one cannot escape dealing with the propositions of natural law. If the question of law and morality is posed as the question of the emancipation of law from the shackles of religion or ethics, this revives the centuries-old battle between natural law and legal positivism. Positivism does not deny the importance of morality, but it does deny that the changing man-made laws are necessarily equated with moral commands, if the latter are understood as superhuman orders or as parts of some universal code.

The problem with natural law is that even an "eternal" or "true" justice changes, as do the theological truths from which so many of the ethical truths are derived. Morality seems to be natural to man; but the other way of stating it, in the form of "natural law," is a concept far too static and inflexible with too little regard for historical and societal changes. It mistakenly assumes a fixed human nature from which natural laws spring. John Rawls is only one of the many who have made desperate efforts to objectivize and positivize the tenets of natural law, but, as with the host of other attempts, his "sense of justice," his "principles of moral psychology," and other precepts seem to fail in his "problem of relative stability" [12] which,

---

[11] Hart, *op. cit.*, p. 181.
[12] John Rawls, *A Theory of Justice* (Cambridge, Mass., 1971).

ultimately, still proposes stable human characteristics, and it does not markedly deviate from the well-known natural law orientations.

The changing nature of the ethical laws does not really call for evidence unless we make the mistake of thinking that we can avoid being mistaken. To refuse to believe in natural law or in a single morality may be a position perilously close to cynicism. Yet belief in an absolute and solitary moral code may indicate a kind of mental thrombosis, and it hints at an idealistic search for the obstinate truth in the arena of values. If Western man believes in the moral value of monogamy this does not make polygamy in other societies immoral. Approval of abortion does not violate the ethical code in one culture just because in another it is defined as murder. Opposite kinds of human behavior—such as homicide and brotherly love, rape and virginity, monogamy and promiscuity, veracity and mendacity, peaceful living together and war —have been virtues, or at least morally approved, at different times in history, their approbation often being attributed to the gods. For example, there were the religious prostitutions in Cyprus and Lydia, the incest practiced within the family of Egyptian pharaohs, and the piracy and legal brigandage of the Crusades in the Middle Ages.[13] Approved immoralities and disapproved moralities are abundant in the social history of man, and one need only look at the changes in ethical values in our own century to question the stability of moral truths.

Morality seems to expand to include natural law beliefs and religious dogmas, at the same time making its connection with law even more complicated. Law itself

[13] Vámbéry, *op. cit.*, p. 8 and *passim*.

is a changing phenomenon, and in its relationship with ethics, law is confronted with another changing phenomenon. Is the law a mirror of moral beliefs, or is morality a reflection of the law? This question of *prius* is of crucial significance. The first alternative holds that only the moral code is valid, and no law in disharmony with it should be regarded as truly binding. The second alternative, following Hobbes and Hegel, proposes the superiority of the man-made law. A third approach would be to understand law and morality in their mutually exclusive autonomy, that is, law as not only emancipated from but independent of ethics.

The philosophy of law was totally dissolved in the philosophy of morals by the ethics of ancient times. Then came the English and French Enlightenment which made great strides toward emancipating law. This was the time when political criminals could start proposing that their crimes were moral deeds and could begin accusing the living law of immoral provisions. In the effort to liberate the human mind from a thousand years of intellectual tyranny, men found it necessary to distinguish between legal and ethical laws. Dante, Machiavelli, Bodin, Grotius, Hobbes, Hume, Bentham, Austin, and of course the Utopians—all claimed morality was subordinate to law, or at least they proclaimed the preeminence of law. As a logical consequence, they attacked the natural law. Essentially their proposal was that law has no necessary relationship with morality, which is not rational and cannot be proved; laws are the command of human beings.

This centuries-old battle has not yet completely succeeded in defeating natural law; there are still sustained offensives against it. To Makarewicz the natural law is the "ideal in law"; it is *selbstverständlich unveränderlich,* evidently unchangeable,[14] and its unchangeable character, as Karl Gareis put it, is its *sine qua non*.[15] Hart can see little difference between the law of gravity and and the Ten Commandments if the observed regularities of nature "were prescribed or decreed by a Divine Governor." [16] Morris Raphael Cohen, in discussing Raffaelle Garofalo's "natural crime," remarked bitterly: "Civilized Italians and Germans at the time that Garofalo wrote might have been shocked at the suggestion that their people would ever be capable of perpetrating the cruelties which Fascists and Nazis have exercised on their opponents or even on innocent children who happened to live in Ethiopian villages or to be of Jewish ancestry." [17] Garofalo's famous belief that "pity" and "probity" are characteristics of all civilized peoples at all times was disproved half a century later: The "tenderness" and "honesty" of the Fascists and Nazis resulted in the torture and death of millions.

There is a conventional notion that morality is concerned with man's internal world, and law with external behavior, which makes a more flexible distinction between positive law and natural morality. When a man violates criminal law norms, he is controlled internally by feelings of remorse or guilt and externally by threat of punishment as applied by another man. Statute books and court practice declare the responsibilities with which law charges human conduct. However, there is no catalog of the re-

---

[14] J. Makarewicz, *Einführung in die Philosophie des Strafrechts auf entwicklungsgeschichtlicher Grundlage* (Stuttgart, 1906), p. 1 and *passim*.

[15] Karl Gareis, *Rechtsenzyklopädie und Methodologie* (2d ed., Stuttgart, 1900), p. 10 and *passim*.

[16] Hart, *op. cit.*, p. 183.

[17] Morris Raphael Cohen, *Reason and Law* (New York, 1961), pp. 34–35.

sponsibilities based on natural law or morality. Legislation decrees the Aristotelian *mala prohibita*, the "prohibited wrongs," proscribed by man-made laws; but there is no official means of listing the *mala per se*, the "wrongs in themselves," prohibited by their intrinsic nature. For instance, it would be unlikely to have a "no smoking" sign in a church to declare that puffing a cigar during services was prohibited. Acts such as this that are *mala per se* are usually vaguely defined or even undefined, but they usually shock other people.

Like many others who unadmittedly have doubts about the strength of natural law, Lon Fuller, who calls himself a "natural lawyer," atttempted to qualify his belief in an unidentified moral designer by confining the relationship between law and ethics to the "internal morality of law." He called this a "procedural version of natural law." His concern was not with the substantive aims of legal rules but with the ways in which "a system of rules for governing human conduct must be constructed and administered." [18] The stability of the moral norms, which is the original and fundamental idea of natural morality, would not be demonstrated through such natural law concepts. Even the neo-Kantian Rudolf Stammler made allowance for changes in morality and natural law; [19] Makarewicz called Stammler's changing content of natural law morality a *contradictio in adiecto*.[20] Stammler identified morality with conscience [21] and proposed the

[18] Fuller, *op. cit.*, pp. 96–97.
[19] Rudolf Stammler, *Wirtschaft und Recht nach der materialistischen Geschichtsanfassung* (5th ed., Leipzig, 1924).
[20] Makarewicz, *op. cit.*, p. 2.
[21] Rudolf Stammler, *Die Lehre von dem richtigen Rechte* (Halle, 1902), pp. 52–92, but also earlier in his *Wirtschaft und Recht*, p. 547 and *passim*

coexistence and collaboration of law and morality in a way already known from Kant's philosophy and, even earlier, from the ideas of Christian Thomasius.[22] But even this "qualified" natural law, which admits changes in its content, may at least partially emancipate law from the chains of theological doctrines.

Rudolf Ihering viewed the law as a form of psychic coercion by the state, by which he meant the punishing power of public opinion.[23] Similarly Gyula Moór proposed that the internal world of the individual was the enforcing power for moral norms which indicate right conduct.[24] These are just attempts to liberate the law norms from the moral rules; the contract between external and internal coercion is dissolved whenever the internal coercion validates itself by external force. Lynching, for example, is a "moral" attempt to compensate for an assumed deficiency in external coercion (the law) through an act based on internal judgment. So also is a prison riot, which attempts to produce "moral" conditions in the otherwise accepted punishment. And so might be the political crime of assassination of a head of state if constitutional procedures had failed to force his resignation.

Other thinkers have carried this line of reasoning even further. Adolf Merkel, for one, found that law and ethics could be equated because the law expresses the common belief of those who live in the same community.[25] How-

[22] Christian Thomasius, *Fundamenta Iuris Naturae et Gentium* (Halle, 1705), vol. 1., ch. 1., pp. 4–6.

[23] Rudolf Ihering, *Der Zweck im Recht* (Leipzig, 1877–1883), vol. 2., pp. 10 and 181.

[24] Gyula Moór, *Macht, Recht, Moral* (Szeged, 1922), pp. 15–16.

[25] Adolf Merkel, *Juristische Encyclopädie* (7th ed., Leipzig, 1922), p. 38.

ever, as Giorgio Del Vecchio maintained, law and morality can be distinguished, but he called it "not a separation, and even less an opposition." [26] There are many common beliefs with little relationship to law, and many laws which are not universally approved. Clashes and encounters between law and morality are very possible, and so their conflict seems as certain as their connection.

In almost all contemporary theories of law, and mainly in the official declarations of the ruling power, it has been claimed that the law is dependent upon ethical systems. This is true even in the materialistic Soviet approach: The chief aim of the courts, as stated in the Regulations on the Soviet Comrades' Courts, is to enforce "communist morality." [27] Even Karl Janka could not deny that law and morality inevitably meet, although he proposed that this is merely a "coincidence" [28] and that they are independent phenomena. Vámbéry ridiculed this argument by showing that since husband and wife are of different sexes, and since altercations take place in marriage, the married partners are thus independent of each other.[29] The dependence of the "independent" law on the moral code was characteristically defended by George Jellinek, who regarded the law as an "ethical minimum," in other words, a guarantee of the preservation of essential moral axioms.[30]

[26] Giorgio Del Vecchio, *Philosophy of Law*, trans. T. O. Martin (Washington, D.C., 1953), p. 276.

[27] F. J. Feldbrugge, *Soviet Criminal Law: General Part* (Leyden, 1964), p. 246.

[28] Karl Janka, *Der Strafrechtliche Nothstand* (Vienna, 1878), p. 139.

[29] Vámbéry, *op. cit.*, p. 39.

[30] Georg Jellinek, *Die Sozialethische Bedeutung von Recht, Unrecht, und Strafe* (Vienna, 1878), p. 42 and *passim*.

The Moral Prescriptions in Criminal Law

Rights and duties—or privileges and responsibilities—as stipulated by law on the one hand and morality on the other have sufficient similarity "to show that their common vocabulary is no accident." [31] This fact unavoidably calls for efforts aimed at approaching the basic theme of morality itself. The similarity in vocabulary invites attempts to see whether it is really a likeness, or maybe only an illusion, and whether law and morality are in harmony or possibly in disagreement. The challenge, so crucially important for understanding the world in which both morality and law operate, is to find an accommodating framework for the prodigious mass of details in the abundantly available definitions of morality. Such a framework could be basic to understanding the problem of crime. Perhaps a kind of operational interpretation of moral values might be reached, although it might be distasteful to those filled with nostalgia for the ideas of natural law and natural morality.

To be sure, anyone approaching the question of morality can scarcely resist repeating Goethe's overquoted words from *Faust*: "Gefühle ist alle"—feeling is all. The logic of gigantism in Goethe's utterance is evident enough to give it the merit of pleasant wisdom and deep simplicity, but it hardly sits comfortably among the cruelties of the real world. Idealism is the art of the "natural moralists," and although they often have far more spectacular ideas than the "positive moralist," they are not so truthful.

[31] Hart, *op. cit.*, p. 168.

George Orwell, in his recently found proposed introduction for the first edition of *Animal Farm*, ventured the statement that "there is now a widespread tendency to argue that one can only defend democracy by totalitarian methods." [32] This odious truth, which seems to hold mainly in times when politically styled criminality is increasingly displayed, leads perhaps to the analogy that "morality," too, as perceived by the ordinary man and as understood in ungarnished everyday thinking (so often resembling religiously based principles), might be achieved only by some kind of powerful and threatening intrusion into man's thinking and understanding. However, in this same writing, Orwell also said that "if you encourage totalitarian methods, the time may come when they will be used against you instead of for you." [33]

And, again with the same corresponding twist, keeping Orwell's prophetic warning in mind, one may contend that this threatening force that "makes" man moral could be easily misused if it resulted only in outwardly practiced behaviors instead of in attitudinal changes. Of course, the possibility of such a blunder of "moral making" may only be minimized, not totally avoided, since no society in the history of man could pride itself with having absolutely no members with only "conformity morality." [34] This seems to be proved by the attitudes and consequential actions of the

[32] George Orwell, "The Freedom of the Press," *The Times Literary Supplement* (London), no. 3,680, Sept. 15, 1972, p. 1038.
[33] *Ibid.*
[34] Richard T. De George in *Soviet Ethics and Morality* (Ann Arbor, Mich., 1969) claims that the actual behavior of the Soviet man shows only a kind of "conformity morality." The distinction between "conformity morality" and "belief morality" resembles Kant's distinction between the external legal and the internal moral conduct. Also it is comparable to the psychological difference between behavior and attitude.

indestructible political criminals. Naturally, the moral-making or moral-teaching intrusive power would prefer "forcing" primarily "belief morality," rather than "conformity morality."

Actually both the morality-making ruling power and the power-opposing political criminal could relish, and in a certain sense be encouraged by the Wittgenstein-initiated "linguistic philosophy" [35] which, to some extent, gives up efforts to develop universally valid absolute definitions and, instead, as is attempted here with the theme of morality, discloses the nature and conditions in which a term like "morality" is used in the understanding of a particular user. If an accommodating definitional-style framework of morality is to be found in order to see its role and place in the realm of the law norms, then, with Ludwig Wittgenstein, one has to say, "Don't ask for the meaning, ask for the use"—since the use of morality, in its end analysis, is its meaning.

In the same vein, Wallace and Walker contend that "the test of a definition of 'moral' or 'morality' cannot be its correctness or incorrectness—but must rather be how well it serves the purposes for which the definition is required." [36] As is widely recognized, the questions about how morality, whatever it may mean, differs from or agrees with the issues of law, are beyond agreement among philosophers (and also among those nonphilosophers who have the courage to enter this province of problems) and perhaps they are beyond the possibility of uncontestable answers. Or better, perhaps, they have too

[35] Ludwig Wittgenstein, *Philosophical Investigations* (Oxford, 1953); "Lecture on Ethics," *Philosophical Review*, 1965; and his other works.

[36] Gerald Wallace and A. D. M. Walker (eds.), Introduction, in *The Definition of Morality* (London, 1970), p. 5 and *passim*.

many answers, all, however, indicating the arbitrary decision or orientation of the responding thinker open to arguments of other respondents.

Indeed, in both philosophical and nonphilosophical areas, confusion has arisen as a result of uncertainty and unclarity about their meaning,[37] and most definitions of morality use terms which themselves are in need of definition. Warnock, for example, suggested that even what Hume and Kant discussed as morality are in fact not analyses of the same phenomenon.[38] This is why, instead of becoming lost in the exitless labyrinth of the definitions of morality, one might understand it better if one simply accepted the undoubted thesis that while, in general, "moral" means approval, "immoral" invites resentment. Or, in other words, the definition of morality may be at least closer approached by defining the "ought." The essential questions, of course, are, Who is the resentor? and Who declares what ought to be done? Or, in the arena of law, What is the role the ruling social-political power and its law play in the development of this "resentment"? and What is it in the ordinary man's mind that makes him believe in the correctness of the conduct that "ought" to be followed?

There seems to be but little disagreement about the desirability of developing a kind of morality in which man believes, rather than to which he simply conforms. After all, "belief morality" promises more security for peaceful living together in society. Even among those who tend to confuse crime, sin, vice, and morality, morality is ideally characterized by a sort of impersonality, which

---

[37] *Ibid.,* p. 1.
[38] G. J. Warnock, *Contemporary Moral Philosophy* (London, 1967), p. 52.

means that even we ourselves should not be exempted from the moral judgments that distribute approvals and resentments.

In the sadly shrinking group of philosophers (modern sarcasm has characterized the contemporary man as one who does not read or think, but only writes), Hare, basically a Kantian, has emphasized this demand for what morality should mean by advancing his concept of "universalizability"; [39] yet he made certain allowances for the pluralism and relative nature of the moral issues. Essentially fighting socially disruptive egoism, he claims that if a person feels a moral commitment that he ought to do something, then anyone else ought to do the same something. This, translated into the language of the problem of political criminality, would mean that the ruling power's law is justified in expecting everyone to follow the declared morality regardless of what anybody may think of the morality of the power. However, Hare also implied that his proposition is applicable only if there are no significant differences between the mentioned "person" and "anyone else" and no relevant differences between their situations. But this would mean a kind of philosophical relief to the political criminal, and to criminals in general —all of whom almost always claim that they are "different" and are in "different" situations.

[39] Richard Mervyn Hare, *The Language of Morals* (Oxford, 1952); "Universalizability," *Proceedings of the Aristotelian Society,* 1954–1955; *Freedom and Reason* (Oxford, 1963); and his other works. His concept of universalizability greatly influenced many modern philosophers. Incidentally, Alasdair Macintyre in "What Morality Is Not," *Philosophy* (1957), p. 325, suspects that Hare has borrowed his terminology from E. A. Gellner's paper on "Ethics and Logic" (*Proceedings of the Aristotelian Society,* 1954–1955, pp. 157–158).

This, however, in itself, would leave the problem of morality—and the immorality of all sorts of criminals— static, unanswered, and unfunctional, or sometimes even disfunctional. On the basis of the Harean pluralistic and relative universalizability, both the ruling power and the law violators could plead the moral nature of their own stand. Therefore, to see morality in its dynamic and functional portrait, one would probably have to add to the "ought" another dimension that would realistically restrict and qualify its relativity without depriving it of its basically and essentally relative character. Without that, as Macintyre posed it,[40] if everyone would judge everyone else by the standard by which he judges himself, a requirement of morality could be converted into a requirement of logic, actually a transition not unfamiliar in moral arguments, which in fact makes the morally important "approval" and "disapproval" of human conduct impossible.

Hare himself apparently has been aware of the vulnerability of using only his criterion of universalizability (essentially a factor in morality that has been claimed ever since mankind used the concept of moral values). So, along with many other thinkers,[41] somehow trying to follow the Kantian "imperatives" (and in this attempt weakening his impressive idea by taking a vacillating dualistic stand), Hare offered for the understanding of the function of morality the element of "prescriptivity." As is widely held by those who are not prepared to dream

[40] Macintyre, *ibid.*, pp. 33–34.
[41] See, among others, P. L. Gardiner, "On Assenting to a Moral Principle," *Proceedings of the Aristotelian Society* (1954–1955); A. Donagan, "Mr. Hare and the Conscientious Nazi," *Philosophical Studies* (1964–1965).

about an unquestionably admirable and ideal universal moral code, and who are reluctant to luxuriate in sentimental yearning for some mysteriously developing "feelings" of moral principles, morality indeed can hardly be conceived as a purposeless phenomenon. And (to take over Hare's proposition but not his dualistic orientation) it can be understood as an *action-guiding force* only as *"prescribed" with a societal goal by powers more powerful than ourselves.*

Sociologists, quite gently, and sometimes not clearly revealing what "learning processes" really means in the mirror of this prescriptivity, call it "socialization" of the members of the society. However, they see, in general, this "prescribing morality" only as "transmitting" culture and only in terms of "learning" values—with a noble impassivity in favor of their oversimplified trust in human nature. Sociologists are sometimes almost obsessed by recognizing man exclusively as a creature who is receptive to "teaching" and as an individual carrier of social conditions, and they refer to him only rarely as also and at the same time a subject of law and social control and an executor of moral values. Such an approach not only deprives the sociologists of the opportunity to come close to the sordid realities of the crime problem, but it reflects their inability to understand the subtle inwardness of forces alien to the orthodox definition of "learning."

Socialization, as so often and conventionally understood by the sociological students of deviance, is apt to conceal the fact that morality and conformity are only particular aspects of man's total responsibility to the lawmaking (and moral-making) social-political power. Instead, his moral value system might perhaps more intelligently be examined and sensed by boldly placing it in

Morality and Political Crime

the more substantial spectrum of prescriptivity.[42] Of course, proposing morality as a "prescribed product" may sound as if it were some Mephistophelian suggestion that would deprive man of controlling his world, but no sophisticated sociological jargon can safely bury the demonic, and as the ultimate yardstick of moral standards, indeed this is what "socialization" really means. The energy that may go into a search for the contrary could only be in the end inescapably rhetorical.

In most sociological-style teachings of this problem,[43] sociologists tend to apply "socialization" as a blanket term, and although they should be credited with having gone some way along the road, apparently they have not gone far enough. They are correct in stating that socialization humanizes the biological organism in order to make it fit into an organized way of life in the society, and they are not mistaken in contending that the family, peer groups, and other interactional agencies offer man guidance and models of behavior. But, by not showing the source of the guidance and models that these agencies transmit, by leaving it unclear that most of these agencies are supposed to carry out this transmission instead of having the discretion not to do so, and by not emphasizing sufficiently, if at all, that this "transmission of culture" is essentially performed with the instruments of reward and punishment—the etiology of socialization in the rather involved sociological presentation does not seem to offer

[42] For a similar view, see Gerhard Haney, *Sozialistisches Recht und Persönlichkeit* (Berlin, 1967); Soltész Márta Katonáné, *Személyiség és jog* (Budapest, 1972); and others.
[43] As a characteristic example, see Leonard Broom and Philip Selznick, *Sociology: A Text with Adapted Readings* (4th ed., New York, 1968), pp. 84–119.

insight into the prescriptive origin and threatening nature of this creative process.

The vagueness of the bases of the tenets and principles that are to be socialized into man and the wooliness of the sociologists' position in looking for the cradle of morality and norms to be transmitted inevitably lock their "socialization" into a not very plausible arena where they fail to show the doubts which may creep into their apparently naturalist-style intellectual world. The same Auguste Comte who gave the name to their discipline could caution them against heavenly justifications in a political society, and consultation of his works could socialize the sociologists toward investigating the origin of the issues to be socialized.[44] Gustav Radbruch too should be listened to; he bitterly admitted that the ideas of the days of yore have been refuted by the realities of our time.[45]

The fact that no human being is able to function in his society without being socialized in itself proves that all *must* accept the rules of the social game. These rules do not just exist without any source. They are prescribed, and the prescriptions are, harshly speaking, commanded by the ruling social-political power. Naturally, this ruling power does not issue detailed orders on how to eat a hamburger, what lies can be told, where to copulate, or when to say a prayer. Yet the ruling power, directly or indirectly, declares a system of moral values, which may change from one ruling power to the next, but which indicates at any given time what conduct is approved and what is resented. Or better, it is a system that makes it relatively

[44] Isidore Auguste Marie François Xavier Comte, *Système de politique positive, ou traité de sociologie* (2d ed., Paris, 1890), vol. 1, p. 361.

[45] Gustav Radbruch, *Mensch im Recht* (2d ed., Göttingen, 1961), p. 37.

clear to all members of the society what behavior is expected of them by the governing power.

All rules of all human conducts, from how to handle a fork or spoon to the prohibition of murder or treason, from apparently insignificant customs to horrible crimes, emanate from this all-embracing system of moral values. All deeds declared as right or wrong, or good or bad, are judged by the system's moral standards, which indicate that the good "ought" to be done and the bad "ought not" to be done. And, incidentally, maybe, the assumption of such a system is the point where the resemblance between logic and ethics seems to be destroyed.

This order of moral rules may not be made up exclusively by the ruling power's own ideas. Moreover, almost always it is mixed and saturated with the thoughts of others and also with traditions. But, in any case, it *is* the social-political power's system, it is the sum total of judgments of moral values or worth that the ruling power wants to prevail, and it is *the* morality that this ruling social-political power prescribes for the sake of the power-designed relationships in the given society. These prescriptions have societal contents, adjusted to the plans and patterns of how the governing power wants to see the society functioning.

The socializing agencies are supposed to be familiar with this system, and they are supposed to transmit this morality to all those whose socialization is in their charge. The prescriptive nature of this system of moral rules is prescriptive also in terms of prescribing that it should be prescribed further to others. Socialization actually means advising another to follow the prescriptions or, if necessary, persuading him to do so with the help of those rewards and punishments whose application is within the prescribed rights of the given socializing agency. The socializing agencies, like all in the society, ought to follow the prescriptions; but these agencies also ought to inculcate what ought to be done and what ought not to be done. If this socialization process is adequate and effective, the prescribed moral principles and issues will not simply be followed, but may be transformed into beliefs. And, if so, they can be further transmitted or prescribed as the true expressions of one's own principles and as integrated parts of the morally structured self. Clearly, in the case of political criminals, or criminals in general, this ultimate goal of the socialization process appears to have failed. But, in turn, if the socialization process fails to develop beliefs, but succeeds in achieving the observance of the prescriptions, crime may be avoided.

Ideally, of course, it is the ruling social-political power's goal that its prescriptions will be "believed" and thus followed easily, without any need to apply forceful instrumental persuasion involving special rewards and punishments. Hamburgers will be eaten, statements will be uttered, copulations will be performed, and prayers will be said at the place and time and in the way that is prescribed as morally approved behavior. Nevertheless, in all known societies the ruling power realizes that, for a variety of reasons, not everybody can be perfectly socialized to the prescribed moral conduct. Not only are beliefs not developed, but even the prescriptions are not followed. Sexual deviances, antireligious actions, robberies, and murders will be committed, political crimes will be perpetrated, and even hamburgers will be consumed in a fashion that might be resented. Some moralities will be expected and requested, based on reason; others will be demanded, based on authority.

The ruling power, then, in the interest of the integrity of the designed moral order, estimates the scale

of the moral values and decides which of the expected
and demanded moralities should be protected with what
kind of consequences to their violation. Some issues will
be seen as morally more important than others, but this
again will depend upon the design of the governing
power's moral system. Some issues (for example, the
unusual consumption of a hamburger, or the telling of an
inconsequential lie) may be simply resented without the
application of any further retorsion on the part of the
ruling power or its agents. Some others (for example, rape
or the disruption of the free practice of religion) may
not only be morally resented but may also prompt the
prescribing authority to express itself through the punitive
action of criminal law.

This has always been so throughout the social history
of man. Confucius established moralities in this fashion
for the Chinese, Moses for the Hebrews, and among other
nations moralities were formulated in the laws of Manu,
in the Code of Hammurabi, or in the books of Zoroaster.
Criminal law, thus, is a protector of morality. In fact,
through the threat of punishment, it reflects the ruling
power's prescriptions, and it may also appear as the
enforcement of the failed socialization.

Man, thus, may find himself in a hybrid world in
which the imaginary and the marvelous are weighted
down by drab and muddy realities and where he must face
difficulties in making a clear distinction between morality
and law. In the course of being "socialized," he soon finds
that, as Barnsley posed it, morals have a "foundation in
reality" and that morality is treated as any other kind of
social fact.[46] He may discover that morality does not

[46] John H. Barnsley, *The Social Reality of Ethics* (London,
1972).

79

represent some eternal set of superhuman rules. It is changing, and he will be exposed to terms such as "legalizing," which in fact means that something "immoral" is made "moral" by the earthly ruling power's law. Even the identity of this power may puzzle him; he may see morality as monolithic because in the course of his socialization he does not really know, or at least he may only vaguely understand, the real sources of the moral rules. Socialization to "morality," which is taught by prescriptions, indicates to him that he is committed to the moral rules. Socialization, as he finds out early, prepares him to subject his aspirations, goals, interests, and views to the moral prescriptions as they were designed by the ruling social-political power, whatever this may mean, in a given social group.

This power not only creates the precepts or maxims to which man gives expression, but also lifts them to the level of overarching moral principles regarded as holding true for all men, whatever their rank or station. After all, morality is a system of *rules* which, according to the prescribing ruling power, should be advantageous for all. Both the adherents to natural morality and contemporary sociologists, at this point, could find ammunition for attempting an assault against the prescriptivity of morality and might cry out and contend that here "morality" is confused with what in ordinary sociology is called "values." This kind of charge, however, can be riposted with the question of what, then, is morality, a term so often and lightly used in sociological writings. The charge could be answered only by returning to times when priest and judge were performing the same social roles, when mores and laws were struggling in the chains of religion, and when any attempt to divorce morality and law was regarded as a hideous sin to be punished. If, as so many claim, to be moral means to live in conformity with human nature, what "human nature" means is still to be clarified.

The position of man in our time, however, is that by learning the beautiful morality he may reap rewards. And the teaching of the moral principles, oddly enough, is backed by sanctions on the part of those who are in charge of teaching him, often even by the threat of punitive criminal law. Following the Hobbesian way of thinking, Hart,[47] Hare,[48] Whiteley,[49] Lundstedt [50] and in general the Scandinavians, and many others—actually a growing group—see these sanctions as a necessary element of the prescriptive and action-guiding moral rules. The sanctions may be anything from social consequences to legal punishments which are apt to develop guilt feelings or remorse in the morality violator and which can warrant his accepting the prescriptions.

In thesi, of course, the prescribed morality could work without the menacing sanctions, and some of the prescriptions indeed often do. But experience has guided all ruling powers at all times in all societies to protect the functional operation of the moral rules with prescribed threatening social and legal consequences. How many of the moral rules are in need of this threat or application of sanctions and how many could function without them, as seen from the social history of man, will vary from one culture to another. For those who appear infatuated with quantifying social truths, one may suggest that they

[47] Hart, *op. cit.*
[48] Hare, *op. cit.*
[49] C. H. Whiteley, "On Defining 'Moral,'" *Analysis* (1959/1960), pp. 141–144.
[50] Anders Vilhelm Lundstedt, *Legal Thinking Revised: My Own Views on Law* (Stockholm, 1956).

count the number of criminal code norms; the stronger the voluntary belief in morality and the weaker the danger of violating the moral rules, the slimmer will be the book of penal statutes.

The potential vulnerability of the prescribed morality is a guide to the lawmaker in declaring as criminal the variety of man's conducts. In this vein Lord Hailsham once said that "the only law which there is any merit in obeying is the one you do not agree with either because you think it is mistaken or because you think it operates against your interest; and the only law which there is any merit in enforcing is the law which at least somebody would not obey if it were not enforced." [51] The criminal code is prepared to react to the failures of the socialization process, the deficiencies of which allow the emergence of dissent from the prescribed morality.

The prescriptive and action-guiding nature of morality, secured by sanctions, can be comprehended as an operational accommodation to the philosophical horizon of realities only if, at the same time, one takes into account the changing source of prescriptions and action guidances and the changing nature of law, and only if one is prepared to accept and absorb changes in the moral rules. Dennis Lloyd, for example, sympathizes with looking at moral values in their rather objective shape, but, he asks, "How, for instance, can we honour with the name of law" the inhuman decrees of the Nazi regime? Yet he admits that "the belief in objective moral values is easier to assert than to justify rationally." Also he admits that "morality is, so to speak, 'secreted in the interstices' of the

---

[51] Lord Hailsham, speaking to Devon magistrates at Exeter on Apr. 15, 1972, quoted by *The Observer* (London), no. 9249, Apr. 16, 1972, p. 3.

legal system, and to that extent is inseparable from it." [52]

It may be a disappointing truth that a "philosophy of life" or a "moral character" dressed up with the concept of good in favorable conditions might be a permanent phenomenon throughout one's whole lifetime, but in the historical perspective it is, most likely, only a transient quality. Although the ruling social-political powers—what a human weakness!—like to be regarded as prophets and tend to design morality for eternity, the mundane world, with another "prophet" coming to rule it, cruelly changes immorals to morals and righteousness to injustice. However, so long as the power is a real power, socialization takes place, and has to take place, according to the design of this power, and the prescriptions have to be regarded as moralities conformable to the power's demands.

If so, criminal law, in general terms, is not a code different from the moral code. Their likeness is not an illusion, and the similarities between their vocabularies are real. The theme of morality is no different from the theme of criminal law. Only the inadequately socialized or missocialized members of the society, who thus do not follow the prescriptions, may therefore feel differently and perceive the world as guiding them to actions not in harmony with the rules of one or both codes. Criminal code and moral code, hence, do not operate and cannot function in disharmony. In a sort of complementary way they run closely together.

If morality is viewed as a power-prescribed action-guiding force, criminal law may be seen as its most significant assistant to secure its validity and maintenance. Their position is not really different from that of

---

[52] Dennis Lloyd. *Introduction to Jurisprudence* (2d ed., London, 1969), pp. 66–67 and 36.

83

international relations where morality in its naturalistic sense indeed never matters. In spite of admirable global efforts one could hardly deny that in actuality there is no power or international police to enforce treaties or other agreements. "If a nation chooses to set treaties aside, and impose its rule on another nation by force of arms, or to invade a neighboring nation on the way to fight another," claims Horatio Dresser, "there is nothing to prevent." [53] And the victor in such conflicts is, of course, always "moral." However, as international affairs may be settled peacefully to the satisfaction of all parties concerned, so morality does not necessarily need the assistance of criminal law. But it may.

This seems to mean that criminal law is a kind of backup instrument in the socialization process, and it comes into operation whenever the state of any moral issue so warrants. The criminal code does not cover all moral rules, but it covers some or many of them—which ones are included depends on the ruling power's judgment about the morally precious nature or vulnerable condition of an issue. Even the simplest conventions have a prescriptive essence. After all, they could not be born without an impregnating source, and calling them customs or folkways could divert attention from the mandatory style of their origin. Even they cannot survive without the help of threatening sanctions: Without sanctions the ruling power's moral code may remain an impotent design.

These conventional moral rules, however, do not seem to invite the participation of criminal law norms, and for the integrity of the moral order the threat of social consequences usually appears to be effective enough. To

---

[53] Horatio W. Dresser, *Ethics in Theory and Application* (New York, 1925), p. 425.

ask someone at a meeting "How are you?" (without being really interested in his welfare) or to say at an introduction to a stranger that "I am pleased to meet you" (without knowing in advance whether this get-together will be pleasant)—such questions are not morally neutral conventions. Their violation may easily lead to disadvantageous resentment. Yet, in view of their relatively low societal significance, in almost all cultures they are allowed to stay outside the sanctioning sphere of criminal law. But betraying one's fatherland, killing someone, taking other people's money, enjoying dangerous drugs, and a long series of other violations do call for the assistance of the criminal code, and this call is made by the ruling social-political power.

Should any society view criminal law as if it were an independent system of norms, so that criminal law and morality could be seen as alienated from each other, then, for example, assaults against the lawmaking ruling power by political criminals could be judged as "morally" justified acts. Also, such a societal view would leave the reason for the existence of law itself unclear, with the chance of comprehending criminal law only as a negative system of provisions without constructive goals. In reality, the sanctions threateningly offered by criminal law can avoid being viewed solely as a magnificent failure in keeping order and can appear meaningful and justified only if they protect and enforce morality.

This asset of the criminal code can, by definition, decorate the criminal law norms with a moral character; it indicates that the norms are vital carriers of the moral prescriptions. To many who so often "feel" and use the words "moral" and "morality," this may seem an excessive claim. But it may be tested against the difficulties inherent in the creation of "natural" morality, a superb and grandi-

85

ose fiction, whose comfortable virtue is that it does not offer compelling conclusions. In their centuries-old great confrontation, however, even connoisseurs of these opposing themes, perhaps mainly those who in our time concern themselves with the problem of crime, sometimes do not make a strong enough attempt to define morality by relating it to the history of ideas that may be recognized as the chronicle of moral issues. Consequently they do not find their way to the unmystic and less abstruse source of moral values.

Consent and Conflict Between Morality and Criminal Law

The perfect socialization of all members of society to the prescribed morality, even if backed by sanctions, borders on practical impossibility. Hence many criminal law provisions will appear to the inadequately socialized as ethically indifferent, or even as guiding them to a conduct they may believe to be immoral. Recognition of this kind of "conflict" between criminal law and morality has intensified efforts to reconcile the quarrel between the natural-morality-based aspirations for a truly natural law and the positive law based on the prescriptivity-characterized realistic morality.

A dualism of natural and positive laws, which could solve the frustrations of the inadequately socialized people's morality as well as that of those who believe in a heavenly justice on earth, however, can function only with irritating logical faults and practical difficulties. Jerome Hall's effort to propose an integrative jurisprudence, where both positivism and natural law would have their place,[54] leaves a dangerous gap where the problems of morality and justice could be argued perpetually. Hall's proposal would justify the ruling power's prescriptions against the politically criminal act, and in essence all crimes attacking the order and peace of the society. At the same time it would justify the political criminal's claim that his act is acceptable because the law is immoral, and in essence all criminals' complaints that their crimes have been caused or precipitated by the immorality of the social conditions. Proposals for this kind of ditheism are actually not new, any more than many other "novelties" in social and criminal sciences that have actually been borrowed from well-known old propositions.

In some systems of dualism, the natural law is claimed to be the source of the positive law; in others it is claimed to be its controlling agent, and sometimes its supplement.[55] Rudolf Stammler's allegorical comment that justice is empty without love and that pity is blind without proper rules [56] reveals his failure to separate law and ethics effectively. Stammler sees hope for harmony between law and morality if both are products of the same culture. In his "four principles of just law" the key to this harmony would be a natural law with changing content or, better, an alliance between the legal and moral worlds. According to Stammler, a just system of law can be achieved only

[54] Jerome Hall, "From Legal Theory to Integrative Jurisprudence," *Cincinnati Law Review,* 33 (1964), p. 153.

[55] Karl Bergbohm, *Jurisprudenz und Rechtsphilosophie* (Leipzig, 1892).

[56] Stammler, *Die Lehre von dem richtigen Rechte, op. cit.,* p. 85. Dennis Lloyd points out (*Introduction to Jurisprudence, op. cit.,* p. 84) that Stammler's idea of a changing natural law is as old as Aristotle's *Nicomachean Ethics.*

87

through morality, and the realization of moral values is possible only with the help of just law. However, Stammler's idea of harmony seems to propose a static culture without legal and moral changes or a changing culture where law and morality would change together from one harmonious union to another. Yet this would be hardly other than a natural law system.

The same problem of harmony disturbed Hare, too, who, as he said, became a moral philosopher because he "was troubled about practical moral questions" [57]—a reputable admission, so rarely heard from thinkers of our time. Certainly, when it comes to the operative problems of morality, any noble thinker must arrive at a sort of schizoid state of mind. While he demands clearly defined moral rules, he cannot believe and cannot accept the use of the same defined moralities for purposes other than his own morality. This turbulence of mind is almost unavoidable.

The source of this evident disharmony, in fact the inconsistencies and shaky views concerning the real meaning of morality, may be found in the conflict between moral issues and law commands and in the confusion in understanding these action-guiding forces. Hare desperately tries to reconcile them, but his recommendation that "we have to make up our own minds about the morality of the king's acts and orders" [58] is apt to defeat his contention for the "prescriptivity" of morality. Also, inevitably, it leads him to a catastrophic dualism, or even pluralism where any morality would be subject to doubt. Hare's anxiety that "the king" may command us to perform what

[57] Richard Mervyn Hare, *Applications of Moral Philosophy* (London, 1972), p. ix.
[58] *Ibid.*, p. 6.

looks like an atrocity, and his question, "Can I be blamed for obeying orders?" [59] may easily draw sympathy for his tortured state of mind about the practical aspects of moral issues. But, at the same time, his proposed dilemma can only deepen the often-sensed conflict between law and morality and, taking it *ad absurdum*, could lead to total disregard for the law and, ultimately, to anarchy. Clearly, no one would seriously assume that Hare meant this end. Yet by allowing "the king's" morality to be questioned on the basis of another morality, he may open up the philosophical avenue for political criminals, and for criminals in general, to commit crimes in the name of their own opposing morality. Similar views can make the justification of crime even easier, for example, Flathman's somewhat reckless statement that "the morality of obligation provides or contributes to stability and order, the morality of ideals and aspirations directs the State toward higher achievements." [60]

The apparent conflict is perhaps not so much between law and morality as between past and present. Law characteristically lags behind morality, or, maybe, morality progresses faster than law. Usually, there is a discrepancy between the time when the ruling power designs the moral order and the time when the lawmakers express this morality and the socializing process enforces it. One may propose that this problem of conflict is actually an "administrative" question. The designing operation of morality is not coordinated with the lawmaking nor with the socializing process so that everything can happen at

---

[59] Hare's talk on the BBC Third Program under the title "Ethics and Politics," also published in *The Listener* (October 1955).

[60] Richard E. Flathman, *Political Obligation* (New York, 1972), p. 318.

the same time to ensure the best opportunity of guiding man's action and to avoid having one morality lagging behind another or having more than one morality in the society.

An example of the common disagreements over law and morality is the famous dispute between Rudolf Ihering and Josef Kohler about Shakespeare's *The Merchant of Venice*.[61] The character of Shylock has been analyzed from a variety of angles. Ihering used him to enter the problem of conflict between law and morality, proving with an irresistible logic that Portia was actually a pettifogging and shrewd advocate against the rights of the law-craving Shylock. Ihering understood the morality of Shylock, who, as a Jew, suffered so much persecution and humiliation in Renaissance Venice. Shylock was a usurer, but not in any criminal sense. Usury was one of the few occupations that the Christian world had left open to Jews, and so his moneylending was not illegal or even immoral in the given world of morality.

When Shylock demanded a pound of Antonio's flesh as the contractual payment for a legitimate debt, Portia accepted the contract as legally binding in the ducal court. Then, in conformity with the Christian morality regarding Jews, she frustrated Shylock by contending that only the flesh should be taken, without spilling a drop of blood, for the contract said nothing about payment of blood. Although Shylock's contract with Antonio, who borrowed 3,000 ducats, contained a condition *contra bonos mores*, it was acceptable under the Venetian law, and he should have been allowed to take the blood with the flesh. If an

---

[61] Rudolf Ihering, *Kampf ums Recht* (Vienna, 1872); Josef Kohler, *Shakespeare vor dem Forum der Jurisprudenz* (Berlin, 1884); cf. also Vámbéry's impressive analysis of the dispute, *op. cit.*, pp. 59–62.

easement is granted to someone to secure a right-of-way over another's property. so Vámbéry's argument runs, he cannot be prohibited from leaving his footprints along the route.[62]

Shylock, the oppressed and humiliated medieval Jew, was struggling for uniform application of the law and contemporary morality, as Ihering was aware. The "Jew of Venice" had faith in the law only so long as he did not understand that the law was an unconditional prescription of morality. His faith ended when the law became the vile power that turned him into a lawless and immoral pariah, depriving him of his claim, property, daughter, and even his religion. Shylock argued for the sanctity of his contract; Portia, however, told him of the "letter of the law," which would make him immoral and guilty of murder if he took his pound of Antonio's flesh. By interpreting morality selectively, Portia exploited Shylock's defenseless social position.

In contrast to Ihering, Kohler found Shylock mean and grasping. (Incidentally, Heinrich Heine considered him the only character in the play worthy of respect.) Kohler admitted that the contract between Antonio and Shylock was legally valid, but with verbose arguments, as shrewd as Portia's, he showed that the verdict against Shylock was really a defense against the immoral use of the law. Kohler apparently ignored Ihering's analysis of the social forces that are crucial in the conflict between law and moral imperatives, and he neglected to consider the universalizability of moral rules. Kohler also ignored the fact that, because Shylock was a Jew, he was not "adequately socialized" and thus could not share the ruling power's moral principles. Kohler, clearly, could not

---

[62] Vámbéry, *ibid.*, p. 59.

understand how morality should be realistically viewed. If he had been able to play the popular television game "To Tell the Truth" when the traditional question was asked: "Will the real Morality please stand up?" he would have seen nothing rise.

It is the paradox of preconceived notions of morality that the many "inadequately socialized" Shylocks of the world, lacking "perfectly socialized" personalities, do not understand or do not accept the ruling power's prescribed morality, since they have their own. It is they who may overturn the power of the ruler and change the meaning of moral ideas. Since lawmaking most often lags behind such changes, the conflict between law and morality in these circumstances is inevitable. Michael Walzer may not have been correct in suggesting that "Machiavelli's adventurer-prince is one of the first of the 'masterless men.' "[63] There are no masterless men. The inadequately socialized person may become the master of any ruling social-political power; he should always be seen as a potential master. It is the self-contradiction of the idea of law that crime may change it, and this is where the political criminal's immorality may be transformed to morality and where the ordinary criminal may become a conformist member of the society. Nevertheless, this should not mean that crime, by changing the law, necessarily helps societal progress or that victorious immoralities bring about better moralities. It should simply indicate a way of social change. The "moral value" may not be seen until centuries later.

No one can deny the moral nature of criminal law as long as a new morality does not overthrow it. In English

[63] Michael Walzer, *The Revolution of the Saints: A Study in the Origins of Radical Politics* (Cambridge, Mass., 1965), p. 9.

and French the word *crime* and in German the word *Verbrechen* mean only a violation of the criminal code. But in Hungarian the word *büntett* means not only a legally prohibited act but also immoral or sinful behavior or an evil fault. No matter what words are used, criminal laws throughout history tend to punish conducts that oppose the ethical norms, and the concept of crime seems unable to dispense with the element of immorality. Theodor Mommsen called attention to the word *crimen* in the Roman law, which meant what was expressed by the earlier word *delictum,* "fault, sinning, an act against morality the fundamentals of which were common to all." [64] Not only was law intertwined with morality in ancient times, but the first law was criminal law, as Sir Henry Sumner Maine proved with historical facts. Mommsen did extensive work on this problem and concluded from his analysis of the concepts of crime, punishment, and responsibility in Roman law that the law was first directed against the violators of community moral obligations.[65]

Among the "crimes first punished by the community," [66] Steinmetz cataloged witchcraft, incest, treason, sacrilege, violations of hunting rules, poisoning, and offenses against sexual morality. Oppenheimer revised the order of this "first" group of crimes: treason, witchcraft, sacrilege and other offenses against religion, incest and

[64] Theodor Mommsen, *Römisches Strafrecht* (Leipzig, 1899), pp. 2–11.

[65] Theodor Mommsen, *Zum ältesten Strafrecht der Kulturvölker* (Leipzig, 1905). Mommsen's questions have been answered by H. Brunner, B. Freudenthal, J. Goldziher, H. F. Hitzig, Th. Noeldeke, H. Oldenberg, G. Roethe, J. Wellhausen, and V. Williamovitz-Moellendorff.

[66] S. R. Steinmetz, *Ethnologische Studien zur ersten Entwicklung der Strafe* (Leiden, 1894).

other sexual offenses, poisoning, and breaches of the rules of hunting.[67] Wake thought that it would be incorrect "to suppose that actions which such peoples declare to be punishable as crimes are so treated because they are thought to be 'immoral,' as we understand the term."[68] However, "moral ideas also may have played a part as early as magic and religion,"[69] and one of the earliest justifications for punishment was violation of the divine law.[70]

Diderot and d'Alembert's *Encyclopédie* (1751–1772) demanded a new moral respect for man and reforms in the criminal law, and the new morality in France resulted in a revolution in criminal law. Typically, first morality changed, and then criminal law. The inadequately socialized men of that time, *now* regarded as enlightened personalities, revolted against the ruling power's moral and legal abuses. The twenty-six-year-old Italian Cesare Bonesana, Marquis of Beccaria,[71] who wrote the "French style in Italian language"[72] so impressively that Hommel said "only the angels" could speak the same, attacked the cruel and repressive criminal law. As Enrico Ferri said,

---

[67] H. Oppenheimer, *The Rationale of Punishment* (London, 1913), p. 71.

[68] C. S. Wake, *The Evolution of Morality* (London, 1878), vol. 1, pp. 293–294.

[69] Maurice Parmelee, *Criminology* (New York, 1918), p. 19.

[70] *Ibid.*, p. 373.

[71] Cesare Bonesana, Marquis de Beccaria, *Dei delitti e delle pene* (Haarlem, 1764), *An Essay on Crimes and Punishments* (trans. from the Italian with commentary by Voltaire, 5th ed., London, 1804). Vietro Verri, deeply interested in philosophy, encouraged Beccaria to write his book. For the circumstances and atmosphere in which Beccaria's work was born, see Marcello T. Maestro, *Voltaire and Beccaria as Reformers of Criminal Law* (New York, 1942).

[72] Vámbéry, *op. cit.*, p. 100.

Beccaria opened a "glorious scientific cycle."[73] But the thinkers of the Enlightenment seemed to know that criminal law cannot be separated from the representation of moral principles.

A humanitarian understanding of crime and pity for the criminal came into being, although sometimes distorted, as in an ordinance of Frederick the Great, who ruled that before an offender was broken on the wheel, the executioner was empowered to strangle him surreptitiously.[74] Montesquieu opposed harsh punishment because it might undermine morality and because he thought that an appeal to moral sentiment would help to prevent crime. Voltaire saw the fear of shame as a deterrent. Beccaria and Bentham emphasized that virtue is its own reward. They all searched for a legal positivism that could counteract the moral negativism thought to be characteristic of criminal law The ferment of ideas about the emancipation of contemporary morality from religion brought the thinkers together on perhaps only one issue: What should be regarded as morally "wrong"? The accusation that philosophers of law tend to neglect the legal aspects of crime and that sociologically oriented criminologists pay but little attention to its moral aspects may be true. Vámbéry was certainly right when he compared them to two groups of wanderers who approach a mountain from two different directions and, having seen only one side of the mountain, nevertheless argue about its overall shape and configuration.[75]

---

[73] Enrico Ferri, *Criminal Sociology*, trans. Joseph I. Kelly and John Lisle (New York, 1967), p. 4.

[74] N. Willenbücher, "Die Strafrechtsphilosophischen Anschauungen Friedrichs des Grossen," *Breslauer Abhandlungen* (1904), vol. 56., p. 23.

[75] Vámbéry, *op. cit.*, p. 145.

Criminologists with an anthropological orientation seem to have avoided a confrontation with the problem of morality, and consequently they have avoided defining crime. Raffaele Garofalo, an *anthropologiste raisonnable*, was one of the few who attempted a definition in his concept of "natural crime." [76] Cesare Lombroso did not even consider the enigma, and so his criminals were not confronted with the problems of morality.[77] August Drähms, one of Lombroso's American adherents, also shunned the issue, although he did strive at a distinction between right and wrong.[78] Vaccaro perhaps preceded Garofalo, and even Durkheim, in working on the concept of public sentiment affronted by the offender's criminal action.[79]

Napoleone Colajanni, one of the most formidable critics of the anthropological orientations, found that anti-individual and antisocial motives were the essence of criminal conduct. It is they that disrupt the peaceful conditions of social life and are contrary to the morality of a given society.[80] Enrico Ferri tended to agree, but with a number of reservations, among them that many immoral and antisocial acts are in fact not punishable.[81] The neospiritualist Gabriel Tarde, one of the most profound minds concerned with crime (although Ferri finds that he was "not a creative genius"), saw crime as closely

[76] Raffaele Garofalo, *Criminology* (Boston, 1914).
[77] Cesare Lombroso, *L'uomo delinquente* (Milano, 1876); *Delittli vecchi e delitti nuovi* (Torino, 1902).
[78] August Drähms, *The Criminal: His Personnel and Environment* (New York, 1900).
[79] M. A. Vaccaro, *Genesi e funzioni delle leggi penali* (Rome, 1889), pp. 154–180, 211–212.
[80] Napoleone Colajanni, *Sociologia criminale* (Catania, 1889), p. 64.
[81] Ferri, *op. cit.*, p. 81.

related to the dominant moral judgment of the society. He rejected Garofalo's conditions of pity and probity; mass killing in a war arouses more pity than any single murder, yet the moral judgment of the social group would not regard the general who commanded the military slaughter as a criminal.[82] The concept of crime is dependent upon the degree of public "alarm and indignation." [83]

Willem Adriaan Bonger approached the definition of crime from the standpoint of historical materialism, but he gave some emphasis to the moral aspects. Crime, he said, is "an immoral act, and one of a serious character." [84] Consistent with his basic political conviction, he defined immoral acts as "those which are harmful to the interests of a group of persons united by the same interests." [85] Thus he ignored the prescriptivity of moral issues and virtually identified immorality with "antisociality," an equally vague or unclear term. Many others, such as Joly,[86] de Baets,[87] Oettingen,[88] and Stursberg,[89]—called by Bonger "the spiritualists" [90]—or Proal [91]—described by Ferri as "eclectic" [92]—strongly emphasized the moral ele-

---

[82] Gabriel Tarde, *La criminalité comparée* (Paris, 1890), p. 186; also see his *La Philosophie pénale* (Paris, 1890).

[83] Gabriel Tarde, 'Misère et criminalité," *Revue philosophique* vol. 29 (1890).

[84] Willem Adriaan Bonger, *Criminality and Economic Conditions*, trans. Henry P. Horton (repr. New York, 1967), p. 379.

[85] *Ibid.*, p. 379.

[86] Henry Joly, *Le crime* (Paris, 1888).

[87] M. de Baets, *L'école d'anthropologie criminelle* (Gand, 1893); *Les influences de la misère sur la criminalité* (Gand, 1895).

[88] Alexander v. Oettingen, *Die Moralstatistik in ihrer Bedeutung für eine Sozialethik* (3d ed., Erlangen, 1882).

[89] H. Stursberg, *Die Zunahme der Vergehen und Verbrechen und ihre Ursachen* (Düsseldorf, 1878).

[90] Bonger, *op. cit.*, pp. xxxi, 199–209.

[91] Louis Proal, *Le crime et la peine* (Paris, 1892).

[92] Ferri, *op. cit.*, p. 82.

ment in the concept of crime; most of them claimed that the immoral is irreligious. Frederick H. Wines, who approached crime from the penological point of view, tried to distinguish crime from sin, but he admitted that they are not mutually exclusive and that moreover most crimes derive from the category of sins.[93]

Statistical methods have been used to approach the problem of consent or conflict between law and moral issues. Such methods represent an attempt to end what Vámbéry called "the uncritical promiscuity of law and morality" [94] while maintaining the moral elements in the concept of criminal law. So-called moral statistics have been used to reach an understanding of crime statistics, and vice versa. Guerry should be mentioned here because he first used the term "moral statistics" and applied cartographic methods to show the state of morals in terms of crimes.[95] Adolphe Quetelet, "the father of statistics," with his "thermic law" tried to find the relationship of crimes to seasonal variations in morals.[96] During the nineteenth century and the beginning of the twentieth, many scholars were occupied with relating moral statistics to social ethics.[97] The moral health of the society is still sometimes

[93] Frederick H. Wines, *Punishment and Reformation* (New York, 1895), pp. 11–13.

[94] Vámbéry, *op. cit.*, p. 82.

[95] André Michael Guerry, *Essai sur la statistique morale* (Paris, 1833); *Statistique morale de l'Angleterre comparée avec la statistique morale de la France* (Paris, 1864). It is a controversial question whether A. M. Guerry and M. de Guerry de Champneuf are the same person; probably they are not.

[96] Adolphe Quetelet, *Sur l'homme et le développement de ses facultés ou essai de physique sociale* (Paris, 1835).

[97] See, among others, Oettingen, *op. cit.*; M. W. Drobisch, *Die moralische Statistik und die Willensfreiheit* (Leipzig, 1867); Georg von Mayr, *Moralstatistik mit Einschluss der Kriminalstatistik* (Tübingen, 1917); Ferdinand Tönnies, "Moralstatistik," in *Handwörterbuch der Staatswiss.* (4th ed., Jena, 1925).

measured in terms of crime. For example, the Federal Bureau of Investigation's *Uniform Crime Reports* suggest that one of the conditions affecting the amount of crime is the existent mores.

Moral elements have been included in the conceptualization of crime by many philosophers of criminal law who believe immorality to be closely identified with crime. In an evolutionary and comparative method, Makarewicz, for example, almost completely identified immoral acts with crime, and moral disapproval with punishment.[98] Franck took a similar position; moreover, he thought morality should be the ideal guide for drafting criminal law.[99] Some thinkers have attempted to substitute a system of social responsibility for moral responsibility because they are averse to the changing terms of morality and are reluctant to admit that a concept of crime exclusive of moral issues has to be exposed to insurmountable difficulties.

Often morals and values, conscience and judgment, and concern and interest are ostensibly confused, and the role of morality is dressed up with seemingly more functional characteristics. This approaches the opinion of the English judges in the eighteenth-century case of *R. V. Wheatley* in which the defendant was accused of defrauding one Richard Webb by delivering to him 16 gallons of amber and charging him for 18. The court refused to regard this as a criminal offense, saying, "What is it to the public whether Richard Webb has, or has not, his eighteen gallons?" [100]

---

[98] Makarewicz, *op. cit.*
[99] A. Franck, *Philosophie du droit pénal* (Paris, 1864).
[100] Cited in P. J. Fitzgerald, *Criminal Law and Punishment* (Oxford, 1962), p. 3.

99

Even Émile Durkheim,[101] in Ferri's words "the most original and the most genuine positivist" of the French sociologists, despite his interest in the moral life of the society, somehow avoided the definition of the problem of morality in criminal law. He believed that law originates in common beliefs and sentiments and that it is actually an index of the strength of the collective conscience.

Many students of the crime problem give no attention to the functional role of morality. Some simply omit it from their conceptualizations, others mention an unexplained "morality," [102] and still others object to including it among the conceptual elements. Indeed not all operate with a version of Baruch Spinoza's theme: We do not frown upon an act because it is a crime, but it is a crime because we disapprove of it. The aversion to or avoidance of any proposed connection between criminal law and morality is attributable not only to memories of eras when religious adherence was enforced by cruel and brutal penal laws. Perplexity may be present also because of an apparent hesitation to take a stand in favor of one or another orientation.

This is characteristic mainly of the sociologically oriented criminology of our time: The problem of morality

[101] Émile Durkheim, *De la division du travail social* (Paris, 1893).

[102] For examples see Robert K. Merton's "moral or institutional regulation" in "Social Structure and Anomie," *American Sociological Review*, 3 (1938), pp. 672–682; or Donald R. Cressey's "moral indignation" in "Crime," Robert K. Merton and Robert A. Nisbet (eds.), *Contemporary Social Problems* (2d ed., New York, 1966), p. 137; or Albert K. Cohen's "moral weakness" or "moral deficiency" in "The Sociology of the Deviant Act: Anomie Theory and Beyond," *American Sociological Review*, 1 (1965), pp. 6–7; or the "moral front" of Walter C. Reckless in *The Crime Problem* (4th ed., New York, 1967), pp. 775–776; and many others.

and criminal law is most frequently missed by those who try to treat the problem of crime. Or, probably, the understanding and explanation of morality, if the term "morality" or "moral" is used at all, do not seem to be particularly appealing to sociological students of crime and deviance.

Although students of deviance sometimes do apply a kind of moral condemnation of crime, yet what they mean by morality most often remains disguised or camouflaged or unclear, and, as it turns out, their moral "stand" apparently is often just an attempt to make sure that crime is covered by "immorality." Maybe their stance for morality is more of an intuition than an argument, but in any case their lavishness in calling attention to all possible "crime factors" is not matched by an equal profusion in explaining this basic component of the crime concept itself.

This display of so many trees with so little woods leaves one to make his own assessment of the views of these thinkers, who seemingly prefer to conceal rather than reveal what they may have intended to express. The wealth of information they offer about crime causation could bear more fruit if we could come closer to the understanding of the concept of crime, morality, and criminal law.

The Immorality of the Political Criminal's Morality

The stand for one or another ethical orientation is a demand against the existing criminal law—unless the moral idea is already clearly represented by the legal norm. It might be a demand for Mosaic justice as a guide for just and equitable behavior or for the Pauline moral law of compensation. It might be a demand for self-realization in the Aristotelian sense or as understood in Aquinas's scholastic ethic. It might be for Immanuel Kant's deontological ethics or for Jeremy Bentham's egoistic hedonism. The Nietzschean values and Bertrand Russell's ethical skepticism are other random examples of the great variety of ethical orientations: Any moral stand may be demanded of criminal law. Actually, however, it would be a demand against criminal law only if the demand were used by the criminal law against others. A moral stand guides the ruling power and the lawmakers to the design and prescriptive definition of moral responsibilities.

"Many and diverse theories have assumed," states van den Haag, "that 'nature' has given prescriptive 'laws' to society and has endowed its individual members with imprescriptable 'natural' rights."[103] But, in reality, the criminal law is the one that operates by charging certain behaviors with moral responsibilities. The values defended by criminal law are ultimately moral issues; they could be fully distinguished from ethical issues only if morality were returned to the province of theology.

A moral system is actually not much different, or strictly speaking not different at all, from a value system, for morality is the source of what is called values. William Graham Sumner's "folkways"[104] are not qualitatively different from his "mores." The difference lies only in the intensity of feelings and the consequent sanctions against their violation. The fact that appropriate dress, table manners, or other folkways are not controlled by criminal

---

[103] Ernest van den Haag, "Moral Rights and the Law," *The Intercollegiate Review*, vol. 8, nos. 1–2 (Winter-Spring 1972), p. 33.
[104] William Graham Sumner, *Folkways* (Boston, 1906).

law indicates that the law may be primarily concerned with the so-called mores. And certainly not all mores are controlled by the commands of the criminal law; man is not made legally responsible for all violations of the morality. However, all criminal law commands contain moral elements, even though sometimes they are almost invisible to the general public, which tends to recognize them only if an immorality arouses significant indignation.

The disorderly parking of a car may be no less immoral than a mass murder. Not only the degree of indignant feelings but the differential severity of the sanctions also testifies to the level of immorality as judged by the given moral system. Nevertheless, fines and the death penalty are not only retorsions; by taking money or the life of the offender, the criminal law also expresses a moral reproach. This moral reproach, an essential part of the moral responsibility-making command, is often overlooked, not only by judges, defense attorneys, public prosecutors, the general public, and the criminal himself, but also by many of those who search for the concept of crime or by many who talk about prison reform or the reformation of the correctional system. As birds cannot be described simply by saying that they are flying animals, and a locomotive cannot be understood just by saying that its engine has power to pull a train, so criminal law cannot be comprehended by referring to it as if it were merely a controlling instrument of the normative system. So prison reform cannot be made acceptable just by ensuring the rights or the comfort of the inmates.

The moral nature of criminal law may be left concealed, but when the moral reproach is admitted to be a component part of criminal law, its moral nature would be difficult to deny. However, the crux of the matter is not so much the existence of morality in criminal law as it is the functional role criminal law plays in making a man responsible for not conforming to the morality of the command. Criminal law may be the product of a variety of social interactions, but, in its ultimate analysis, it is a prescription, the "command of the sovereign," that is, the commanding prescription of the social-political power. This power takes a stand for a certain morality and demands its acceptance.

Morality is not the product of law; the law exists to enforce the morality. Parking by a hydrant is wrong, killing people is wrong, and thus criminal laws had to be made to promote orderly parking and respect for other people's lives. Criminal law is not only a regulative tool, as is often mistakenly assumed by those who handle norm systems, but it is primarily a teleological instrument in the service of the moral design of the society as designated by the ruling power. The members of a society are necessarily required to live in accordance with the "command of the sovereign," who threatens to hold them responsible for any deviation; this ruling social-political power makes all efforts to this end, and criminal law is part of the ruler's arsenal. The power attempts to inculate a whole society with its particular brand of morality. This strange and indiscriminately cruel positivism is hard to describe, mainly because the belief in the myth of some kind of "natural morality" still seems to survive long after it has become extinct in reality by being emancipated from its religious master. Even the ruling power has ideals, but it does not have illusions, and "the presence of a Law Giver in a society appears to be a causal condition of the genesis of morality." [105]

[105] Geoffrey Russell Grice, *The Grounds of Moral Judgement* (Cambridge, 1967), p. 118.

Morality and Political Crime

The importance of this aspect does not rest on details of interpretation or beliefs, but on the question of its functional nature. Moral responsibility making is not an isolated factor at any given time. It explains crime and relates criminals to conformists in spatial, cultural, and time dimensions.[106] The history of crime reveals differing approaches to morality, and accordingly, to the definition of moral responsibility. No particular definition of moral responsibility has ever seemed right to all members of a society—how else could political criminals emerge? But who is responsibile for what, and why? The answer to this question can lead to an understanding of the moral system of the sovereign power. Moral responsibility will never be perfectly conceptualized or even well understood. Its significance in the philosophy of crime lies in the very fact that it is relative.

By determining the moral system, the lawmaking ruling social-political power helps secure and maintain group order. In this context the morality, and making the members of the society responsible for following it, is functional in nature; therefore it cannot operate in an atmosphere of stiff formalism. For the morality-commanding law to be respected and observed, it has to operate within the concept of *free will*, a problem that may be an obstacle to an understanding and conceptualization of *dual responsibility*, as well as the responsibility of morality, which actually are identical; the responsibility with which criminal law charges certain conducts and the responsibility that refers to factors that lead an individual to act counter to the command.

The problem of free will is one of the most difficult

[106] Schafer, Stephen, *The Victim and His Criminal: A Study in Functional Responsibility* (New York, 1968), p. 138 and *passim*.

and yet most popular in philosophy, but in the areas of sociology and criminology it is almost completely neglected. Immanuel Kant bitterly complained that a thousand years' work had been expended in vain on its solution. Nicolai Hartmann admitted that we cannot even hope for a satisfactory answer. The debate on the controversial issue of determinism and indeterminism, an interminable series of arguments, is the focus of the problem. It appears that acceptance of an unlimited application of the law of causality would be as grandiose a hypothesis as taking the freedom of the will to be merely a metaphysical concept.

The notion that man has no free choice and that his acts are fully determined by external forces, that is, determinism, would annihilate the idea of human will. Determinism would suggest that it was not a political criminal's "will" that motivated his action, but that his crime was some sort of automatic offense caused by outside forces. Strangely, however, indeterminism leads to the same conclusion: A will that is not involved with causal reality would be only an illusion. Joannes Buridanus's donkey, also mentioned by Schopenhauer, Windelband, Gomperz, and others, illustrates the complex nature of arguments between determinism and indeterminism and serves to defend as well as to attack both views. A hungry donkey stands between two haystacks, equally fragrant, equal in size, and equally distant. The unfortunate animal, having no will to decide (if the deterministic view is correct), or having no motives to influence its decision (if the indeterministic orientation is right), eventually becomes absolutely indifferent and thus dies of hunger. This classic story also makes clear that the validity of one's conclusion rests upon what one actually understands by the terms that are used.

Since nothing new can be said on the problems of

morality and free will, and any new theory, if carefully examined, proves to be only a version of one of the old theories, the chances of reaching a solution are slim. Therefore, at least for understanding the practical application of the question of the freedom of the will, a compromise might be necessary because there is no philosophical guarantee either that adherents of the indeterministic view have freedom of will to arrive at their conclusion or that adherents of the deterministic idea express their evaluation only as mouthpieces of external forces.

All criminal laws seem at first to be strongly indeterministic. The idea of punishment itself indicates the lawmakers' assumption that the criminal has a freedom of choice and may choose the morals and, accordingly, the moral or immoral behavior he prefers. Criminal law assumes that man is able to form a "more or less impartial judgment of the alternative actions" and can act in conformity with this decision or valuation.[107] It would be senseless, so the argument runs, to offer a choice between reward and punishment if free will were not a fact. How else, it is said, could we praise the conformist citizen and convict the criminal if this were rejected. After all, criminal or moral responsibility is based on having the choice to commit an immoral criminal act. Criminal law operates on the assumption that man is an intelligent and reasoning creature who can recognize moral issues. In other words, only those can be punished who "want" to commit a crime. Our penal systems do not dispute this point, and although we like to mislead ourselves by preaching "correction" and "rehabilitation," no rethinking has set aside the concepts of guilt retribution, and deterrence.

[107] Morris Ginsberg, *On Justice in Society* (Harmondsworth, 1965), p. 168.

The freedom of will, something that we tend to be so proud of, is not always as free as it appears. In reality this freedom refers to only a limited range of choices, and among these choices there is only a limited number of alternatives, and even here biological needs may have a role in determining the action. But the Kantian dualism does not seem to fit in with any mixture of deterministic and indeterministic orientations; the realistic human will can exist alone neither in the causal nature nor in the intellect. The *mundus sensibilis* and *mundus intelligibilis,* man's two worlds, as separate entities cannot be acceptable by any moderate yet one-sided belief in free will. In our functioning and changing universe, man's position claims the merger of these two worlds. The morality of these merged worlds molds and shapes both the causal reality and the intellect into a single unity. This morality is not some "Third Reich," as Heinrich Rickert called it;[108] it is not a self-contained third world that can be linked with the other two. Also, it has but little connection with Hegel's strict historical and social causality, where the realities of nature, "the unsolved contradiction," [109] cannot find their comfortable place.

The moral system of the culture both saturates and limits individual will. It is a "real world" in which the individual lives and functions, and he learns (or better, has to learn) to do so through the socializing process. Morality is not only built into the person, but it also builds his personality and thus limits his choice and sets his alternatives. Wallace and Walker contend that "even when a

[108] Heinrich Rickert, *System der Philosophie* (Tübingen, 1921), vol. I., p. 254.

[109] "Unaufgelöste Widerspruch," in Georg Wilhelm Hegel, *Encyclopädie der philosophischen Wissenschaften* (Leipzig, 1923), p. 209.

man has acted in accordance with his moral principles and has done what, in his view, was morally right, he is not immune from criticism; we may criticize a man although he thinks that he acted rightly." [110] The socializing process instills man's prejudices, likes and dislikes, beliefs and disbeliefs, affirmations and negations, approvals and resentments. Socialization, that is, prescribed socialization, makes the individual what he is. Man actively masters his culture, but only after he has passively accepted it.

Except, perhaps, where physical necessities, which prevail throughout the material universe, rigidly and irresistibly dictate human action, our faculties of knowing, reasoning, choosing, and deciding are almost exclusively arrested by indoctrination in the morality of our culture. Therefore these faculties, all related to the will, are not really free. Man knows, reasons, and makes his choices, but normally what he would will to know, what he would will to reason, and what choices he would will to make are acts limited by the moral ideas prescribed for his culture. This is why the more a person is socialized, the more likely he is to be a conformist. Socialization and resocialization are operational concepts applied to the problem of free will.

Those who argue against punishing the political criminal severely, or against the idea of retribution in modern penal systems, might take as their motto Jean-Paul Sartre's cynical remark that "I am responsible for everything, in fact, except for my very responsibility." [111] The morally-culturally imbued and limited will mirrors the functional responsibility. The moral system not only establishes the direction and range of knowing, reasoning, and deciding,

---

[110] Wallace and Walker, *op. cit.*, p. 7.
[111] Jean-Paul Sartre, *Being and Nothingness* trans. Hazel E. Barnes (New York, 1956), p. 555.

but also cautions man to make these faculties function in the prescribed direction and within the prescribed range. While there are these chains on the freedom of man's will, the ruling power expects that what freedom there is will be used. Man is made responsible for functioning outside the approved limits and for trespassing on the prescribed range. At the same time, he has the responsibility to make his will function within these approved limits in order to promote his culture.

When man functions within his limited freedom, this is expected, and possibly rewarded; when he functions outside the boundaries, this is resented, and possibly punished. This does not mean that all who are inadequately socialized and who, as a result, feel less restricted in their freedom of will, and whose freer wills may even choose illegitimate or immoral alternatives, are necessarily criminals. However, such leaking freedom of will creates the possibility of revolt against the social-political power.

Nevertheless, at the same time, man is not condemned to passivity. He is supposed to use his knowledge, reason, and ability to choose and decide in order to safeguard, improve, and perpetuate his prescribed morality. He is expected to be functional; moreover, he can even be made responsible for that. The Leninian thesis that he who does not work should not eat is understandably not accepted in all cultures. But in all societies man is taught to have aspirations and goals, yet only for his culture and not against its moral values. His functional role extends as far as the confines of his freedom of will. A culturally-morally imbued and limited free will based on functional responsibility testifies to the fact that we are taught only what we need to know in order to participate in our particular societal group. The ruling power of this group designs and defines the values to be learned and establishes the degree to which the will is to be inculcated and limited by the prescribed moral system.

The operation of any power may well lead to the development of an opposing force that may be capable ultimately of taking over the rule and changing the system of morality. Political criminals are not always the losers. The dynamics of such a change would depend largely on the potential of those who are inadequately socialized and who might thus use their greater freedom of will to make choices outside the morally limited area. The change might also depend on the degree of discomfort caused by the moral values introduced by the potential new power structure. Those who were adequately socialized under the original power might not feel discomfort because of the limitations previously imposed on their knowledge and reasoning.

The potential for change may come from the inadequately socialized man also because his emotions can play a role in his reasoning and decision making. While the adequately socialized man is expected to control his emotions, the inadequately socialized is more open to the influence of emotional forces. Emotions may arouse as biological drives do; however, while the latter become activated by the needs of the physical organism, the development of emotions is largely dependent upon how man perceives his situation. Since the inadequately socialized individual has not fully learned the ruling power's moral values and thus does not and cannot meet the demands of the "sovereign," he perceives his societal circumstances in a profile different from what is expected by the social-political power. His consequent broader freedom of will, therefore, not only offers him room for counterbeliefs, but is also apt to arouse accompanying anxiety, anger, hostility, or other emotions over the threat to the worth of his self, his morality, and his society, as he views them.

The threat of being punished by criminal law, or better, the element of sanction in the definition of morality, can reinforce or fortify the emotional aspects of the inadequately socialized person's antagonistic beliefs. These emotions can markedly energize him toward a more complete and rather more energetic expression of his immorality (which he thinks is morality) as a response to the governing morality (which he thinks is immorality). His inadequate empathy for moral prescriptions and his failure to develop adjustive patterns to conform with the sovereign's moral principles upset his psychic equilibrium—or rather, the prescriptivity results in excitability in such a person. This is why the political criminal tends to neglect arguments at a round table and, instead, resorts to excited emotional confrontations with the ruling power, whose morality is seen by him as a manifestation of the sovereign's immorality. His emotions are not really caused by a Freudian sublimation of primitive or infantile instinctual drives, but by a misunderstanding or nonunderstanding of moral issues as they were designed and defined, partially through the criminal law, by the designer and definer of his social group.

When the political criminal is successful in his action, a new morality and new norms may be created, and the old morality and old norms may be rejected or reversed. The content of prescriptivity may change. If so, an extension of the socialization or even a resocialization is unavoidable. The ruling power's morality will be regarded as immorality, and the political criminal's immorality will become the moral system. However, so long as the existing social-political power prevails, the original moral goals and aspirations obtain, regardless of the inadequately socialized person's differing views. The sovereign's ideas and beliefs are fortified, limitations on freedom of the will remain unchanged, and the designed roles of men continue with the same assigned functional responsibilities. In other words, continued socialization takes place according to the morality and societal design of the existing power. Since man's will is not entirely free, aspirations and goals are seen as legitimate, barriers to them justifiable, and roles constructive.

The political criminal—or a criminal of any sort— is not necessarily ignorant, in spite of his inadequate socialization. He is aware of the ruling power's morality in terms of its prescriptive nature and its sanctions. But, because he is inadequately socialized, he does not and perhaps cannot believe in it, and, thus, in his action he is not guided by it. Too, he is ready to violate this dominating morality, even at the price of suffering the sanction, without being capable of developing regret, remorse, or the feeling of guilt, and with the capability of being convinced that his immoral conduct is moral. No wonder we are indeed "immoral" in the judgment of certain others unless we can force those others to give up their believed morality and accept ours. Nevertheless, the criminal law command is trying to force these others to observe our principles, and, as Lloyd pointed out, "Once the rule is laid down or determined, it does not cease to be law because it may be said or shown to be in conflict" [112] with others' morality

Hart rightly contends that moral judgments cannot

---

[112] Lloyd, *Introduction to Jurisprudence, op. cit.,* p. 37.

be established or defended, as statements of facts can, by rational argument, evidence, or proof.[113] But this is not really necessary; the evidence or proof is the law itself, and, as Hobbes and Austin correctly claimed, no law which is in fact an expression of the morality can be "legally" unjust. The inadequately socialized individual, who enjoys an undesigned and exceptional expression of freedom of will, may thus have preferences drawn perhaps from other cultures, which are not in conformity with the prescribed morality. Yet, by definition, his preference is necessarily immoral so long as the criminal law does not approve it. The political criminal, on the basis of the general characterization of the concept of morality, may claim the moral nature of his act by contending that "his cause" prescribed and guided his action. Since his cause disagrees with the cause of the ruling social-political power, however, he is just plotting, to use an English legalistic term, a "conspiracy to corrupt" the prescribed morals, and, consequently, however positivist the political criminal's morality may sound, it can only be considered immorality.

Since the political criminal, and the criminal in general, in view of his inadequate socialization, does not comprehend the morality behind the criminal law norm, if he does not express *his* morality against *the* morality in a criminal fashion, it is the fear of punishment rather than respect for the harmony of the moral and criminal codes that stimulates him to the observance of the command. His crime, thus, in essence, is not really an act of moral opposition against the norm-forming power, because in the ultimate analysis he is not moral and cannot even

[113] H. L. A. Hart, "Positivism and the Separation of Law and Morals," *Harvard Law Review*, 71 (1958), pp. 601–602.

know what morality is, and he cannot evaluate or judge the values of the prevailing morality. Rather, the law appears to him as an alien and external phenomenon with which he is unfamiliar and whose moral rationale is incomprehensible.

Political crime, and crime in general, seen in terms of revolt against the ruling power makes sense only if the criminal understands the values on which the norms are based. In most instances, however, he knows the formal norms and is aware of what can and cannot be done, but because he lacks adequate moral saturation, he cannot be acquainted with the moral issues or moral values underlying the norms. He knows the formal prohibition, and being in possession of his own immoral morality, he is able to rationalize his own deviation. He knows that treason, murder, rape, and shoplifting are prohibited and are declared immoral acts, but he does not understand why. Yet without this understanding the criminal can form only a phenomenalistic judgment whereby the world appears to operate without rhyme or reason and in an arbitrary manner that leaves him at its mercy.

The assumption that criminals have more freedom of will, and use illegitimate means to achieve blocked goals, does not provide a solution to the crime problem. Limitations on the freedom of will do not exclude goals and aspirations, and restrictions on morality do not prohibit interpretative changes in moral issues. Moreover, aspiration and moral improvements are functional roles of man if kept within limits. All human beings have goals, many want changes in morality, not all of which can be achieved or would be permitted. Why, then, have not all people, rather than only a fraction of them, turned to illegitimate alternatives?

Crime has existed since the dawn of history, and all crimes have been committed because of blocked aspirations, whether political, economic, intellectual, communal, or sexual. Moreover, it may be said that the whole course of personality development, from infancy to later life, has always been based on learning to strive for certain morally approved cultural goals and learning to live with frustration if the goals, however moral, are unattainable. This learning process and the frustrations that sometimes result are a necessary part of group membership.

Even in primitive societies which practiced individual revenge or blood feud, the "offender" did not attack his victim because of some inherent drive for violence, but because the victim had something he wanted—food, the skin of a special animal, a precious stone, or perhaps even the status that goes with power and success—that could not be obtained as easily in another way. Criminals have always been goal-oriented. The criminal of today is not basically different from the criminal of any other period. Only his aspirations and the limitations on his freedom of will change from time to time and from place to place. His socialization is more organized now than it was in the past, his ruling social-political power has become more centralized and institutionalized, but all changes are attributable only to the moral definitions of his era and society.

Inadequate socialization results in a misunderstanding of moral prescriptions and in a lack of constructive ambitions: A "rolelessness" may develop, meaning here the role that is expected by the sovereign's moral command. But, because of his inadequate socialization and thus faulty aspirations, the criminal cannot determine which rights and duties are his, and the political criminal cannot judge the morality of the moral prescriptions. He cannot see the justification of his functional role, and so he cannot identify the constructive role he would otherwise play in the service of the sovereign's system.

Given this roleless state, the political criminal, and the criminal in general, unable to recognize the positive values expected of him, cannot form the expected positive aspirations. If the political criminal, or the ordinary offender, turns to destructive actions, this is perhaps not so much a matter of choice among alternatives as an option available to him in the absence of his positive moral system.

In no known society are privileges and prohibitions evenly distributed, and the question of distribution depends on the desire of the ruling power, as expressed, for example, by the law. Since all laws are formulated on the unspoken assumption that they are just, although they may not appear so to all members of a society, particularly the inadequately socialized, the "morality" of the political criminal's immorality may be understandable, but from the point of view of the ruling power's moral prescriptions, it is unacceptable.

4

Concepts of the Political Criminal

The Powerful and the Powerless

Among the few thinkers who have attempted to conceptualize political crime or the political criminal, one group has tried to approach the problem from a structural point of view by contrasting the powerful in any given society with the powerless. By posing the question in this framework, essentially an Austinian idea, they are actually coming close to the salient notion of crime and morality, since it is but logical that only the powerful is in the position to define certain human behaviors as crimes and to decide what moral principles are to be followed, and only the powerless can want to change the prevailing law and morality by turning against the powerful.

This approach may also be understood to imply that the powerful is guilty of some political crimes against the powerless who, in turn, may be seen as victims. It may further imply that the victimized powerless could be

119

"morally" justified in seeking redress in the form of political crimes against the "guilty" powerful. However, in addition to the fact that by definition the powerful cannot be charged with immorality or guilt so long as it is the powerful, the logic of the idea of the "guilty powerful" seems to fail by neglecting the cumulative outcome of a trial where the powerless might seat the powerful in the dock. Should the accusation against the powerful succeed, only the power structure would change in favor of the powerless, but the basic characteristics of the relationship between powerful and powerless would not be altered. It would be hard to imagine a new powerful (that is, the former powerless) that would not want to dictate a legal and moral order against the new powerless (that is, the former powerful).

The truth of this thesis has been experienced throughout the social history of man, most frequently in the discomforting extravaganza of the last half-century, whenever power changes and social changes have taken place, and it does not seem to need further evidence. Perhaps those idealistic honest souls who still believe in the vanished innocence of our world and who still struggle with their desperate impulse to dream become progressively more difficult to convince with such a proposition. But nobody who is ready to dive under the surface of the apparently gentlemanly fair plays could deny that it expresses the truth of the real and ruthless events in man's universe, however disillusioning it may sound. It is just one of the reminders of the profound complexity of "justice."

Franklin H. Giddings, who introduced the English translation of Louis Proal's book *Political Crime*, contends that one of the meanings of the term political crime "is that of the crimes perpetrated by governments for alleged reasons of state and by politicians for alleged reasons of expediency or for political advantage."[1] He claims that this agrees with Proal's approach to the concept of political criminality, which begins with the history of Machiavellism and deals with anarchy, assassinations, and the corruption of law and justice, through criticism of political leaders, churchmen, and moralists.

Giddings suggests that politics without morality is the ruin of society, just as "science without conscience" (originally said by Rabelais) can destroy the soul. Although Proal selected his examples from European chronicles, Giddings suggests that the American scene, with its political aggressions, intimidations, and corruption, can also furnish illustrations that support his stand, which can be understood in hardly any other terms than the popular "natural morality," with a recognizable overtone of sentimentality for the underdog victims of political or social unfairness.

Raffaele Garofalo, in his renowned *Criminology*,[2] gave the impression that he too viewed political crime in the powerful versus powerless context, although he did so somewhat covertly, directing his allusions primarily toward the sympathy for the powerless in a societal mirror. Faithful to his "rationale of the natural crime," where the community's average altruistic sentiments of "pity" and "probity" would be the prerequisites to qualify an act as crime,[3] he states that the "purely political crime" has

---

[1] Franklin H. Giddings, Introduction to Proal's *Political Crime* (New York, 1898), pp. v–vi.

[2] Raffaele Garofalo, *Criminology* (Boston, 1914) (first published in Italian in Naples in 1885; Garofalo himself translated it into French; the English version was translated from this French edition).

[3] *Ibid.*, p. 33.

nothing to do with "true criminality." [4] He did not reach this conclusion without hesitancy, and admitted that "the subject of political crimes presents difficulties of a most serious character." "How are we to contend that conspiracy or rebellion against a lawful government is not a true crime?" he asked, "Can there be anything more dangerous to the particular society?" [5]

Garofalo, who failed to distinguish morality from sentiment, or, maybe, tended to assume that sentiments have a function in forming moral principles, excluded "from the field of criminality" acts which menace the state as a governmental organization, political rioting, meetings to conspire against the government, affiliation with revolutionary sects or anticonstitutional parties, inciting to civil war, resistance to officers of the law, injury to the public peace or to the political rights of the citizens, election intrigues, illegal arrests, acts which contravene the local or special legislation of a given country, unlawful carrying of arms, infringements of laws relating to railroads, and others which are ordinarily interpreted as political crimes or sabotage offenses.[6] Although he suggested that "love of country" is a noble sentiment, Garofalo thought that to prefer a foreign country to one's own or to fail to be moved to tears at the sight of the national emblem does not make a person a criminal. If a person disobeys his government or accepts employment "at the hands" of a foreign power, he may be "a bad citizen, but not a bad man." [7]

Following Darwin's and Spencer's ideas, Garofalo believed in a "moral sense," expected of all men as if it

[4] *Ibid.*, p. 185.
[5] *Ibid.*, p. 37.
[6] *Ibid.*, pp. 41–42.
[7] *Ibid.*, pp. 15–16.

were a sociologically explainable psychological phenomenon. The absence of this moral sense, he contended, makes an individual a criminal person, since its lack hurts other people's sentiments for pity and probity. As Garofalo stated, this is an anomaly of the moral sense. However, this human quality "which evolution has rendered almost universal" cannot be declared absent in political criminals; therefore, their lawbreakings or disobediences that do not violate the altruistic sentiments cannot be regarded as crimes.

Garofalo, and here enters his "powerful versus powerless" notion, did not oppose stamping out these "noncriminal offenses," and he understood the use of stern measures against them, mainly because they intimidate the state authority and because the threat of severe punishment might intimidate would-be political criminals. Yet he could not see political crimes as immoral acts and could not include them in his definition of "natural crime." [8] Also, this is why he did not incorporate political crimes in his suggested "international penal code" [9] and did not refer to political criminals among those offenders who should be eliminated or excluded from society. Instead, he proposed a 'Code of Disobediences" to be formulated by each state according to its individual necessities. Unmistakably, this guided him to contradictions in his interpretation of sentiments and led him to a scenario of squabbles over his trying to capture the concept of morality but being unable to hold onto his general understanding of crime. By detaching political criminals from his pivotal definitional element of moral sense, Garofalo is left conceiving them as the powerless who got into

[8] *Ibid.*, pp. 45, 127, and 401.
[9] *Ibid.*, pp. 403–416.

conflict with the powerful, but he does not attribute to either of them moral moral fortitude and does not expect the public's altruistic sentiments to be aroused either for or against them.

Another of the classical thinkers who viewed political criminals as the powerless in the social structure was the Dutch lawyer and publicist, a founder of the International Union of Penal law, Willem Adriaan Bonger, who spelled out his stance in *Criminality and Economic Conditions* [10] but again from another angle of understanding.[11] He commented voluminously on a number of criminological writers and presented one of the most penetrating studies of the field before he was truly on his way in discussing political crimes—perhaps an ideological summary of all he thought about the crime problem in general. Bonger's view on political criminals is not simply a profile that contrasts the powerful with the powerless, but an attempt to get behind this structural fact and develop a model which ought to enable him not merely to describe, but also to explain and understand. His identifying the powerless with "the oppressed class" and political crime with breaking "the political power of the ruling class," and his calling the political criminal a *homo nobilis* who reflected economic conditions—all indicate that his moral defense of political offenders is in a Marxist perspective, a framework he proposed as the basis for his analysis.

Bonger suggests that those who monopolize the state power defend their position by the threat of severe penalties, and since the dominating ruling class does all that is necessary to maintain its position unimpaired, political

---

[10] Willem Adriaan Bonger, *Criminality and Economic Conditions* (repr. New York, 1967) (translation based on the original, published in Amsterdam in 1905).

[11] *Ibid.*, pp. 648–655.

crimes necessarily emerge if and when economic and social development lags behind or runs ahead of political development. Since the liberty of the oppressed class is restricted and the chances for changing the situation by legal means are slight, there is a "danger that one of those oppressed will kill the autocrat, either to better the situation or to take revenge for what he and his have suffered." [12]

Bonger contends, thus, that those who commit this kind of crime for these reasons have nothing in common with ordinary criminals except that both are called criminals. To Bonger the only socially just solution of the crime problem would seem to be to alter the capitalistic economic system that weakens "social feelings" and has a "preponderant, even decisive" role in criminality.[13] He refers to Tarnowsky [14] and Wadler [15] in using Russia as an example, where political crimes were only acts of defense against the cruelty and violence of the government toward the oppressed people; naturally, his reference was to the Russia before the Soviet Union eliminated the capitalistic economic structure.

Anarchists, in Bonger's analysis, represent a subgroup of political criminals who do not find a comfortable place in his Marxist-type category, "great political criminality." They abhor discipline and militarism, even if regimentation is required for the support of a party. Therefore, anarchists, who are in Bonger's view excitable, vain, and ignorant, having "no clear idea of any theory whatever,"

---

[12] *Ibid.*, p. 649.
[13] *Ibid.*, ch. 7 in Book 2, "Conclusions," pp. 667–672.
[14] E. Tarnowsky, "Les crimes politiques en Russie," *Archives d'anthropologie criminelle*, 12.
[15] A. Wadler, "Die politische Verbrechen in Russland," *Zeitschrift für das gesamte Strafrechtswissenschaft*, 29.

do not help evolutionary-revolutionary changes in the economic system, and consequently, do not contribute to the combat against crime. In the modern literature, Marshall B. Clinard and Richard Quinney refer to "violations which occur in the course of the attempt to protest, express beliefs about, or alter in some way the existing social structure." Although it is not quite clear what they mean, the statement perhaps fits into Bonger's views on anarchists or similar lawbreakers.[16] His refined concept of political criminality distinctly identifies acts against the capitalistic ruling power not only in the Marxist but even in the Marxist-Leninist sense. Maxwell was thinking in the same vein when he distinguished between *rétrograde* and *antérograde* offenders, the latter meaning those who find the socioeconomic evolution too slow.[17]

The Achilles heel in Bonger's argument, which acquits the innocent political criminal and makes the social-political power guilty, is essentially not much different from that of others who similarly contrasted the powerful and the powerless, and thereby made themselves vulnerable to the risky conceptualization of morality. Bonger, covertly though, proposed a denial of the pluralistic nature of moral issues. And while he rebelled against the fact that the ruling power gives its manifestations irrefutable authority by detaching them from ethical scrutiny (as Bonger interpreted ethics), Bonger did not recognize that should the power he desired take over the rule (even if this change were some act of fate or historical destiny),

[16] Marshall B. Clinard and Richard Quinney, *Criminal Behavior Systems: A Typology* (New York, 1967), pp. 177–187; their selected bibliography (pp. 187–189) extends only to the last three decades and only to American references.

[17] J. Maxwell, *Le concept social du crime* (Paris, 1914), p. 52.

the new power would not have the option of acting differently in the arena of wrestling forces. The powerful and the powerless would confront each other again, and only the tenets of morality would take another prescriptive direction.

The Honest and the Corrupt

Another group of thinkers have attempted to conceptualize political crime by opposing the honest and the corrupt. Actually they again contraposition the powerless with the powerful, yet with less emphasis on their stations in the social structure and with almost no comparison of apparently different moralities. When they dress up the honest powerless with upright truthfulness and trust in the declared moral principles, and the corrupt powerful with moral perversion and ethical malpractices, they do not operate with the conflict between the "right" morality of the honest and the "wrong" morality of the corrupt; rather, they charge the corrupt powerful with hypocrisy and double standards.

While Bonger and others did not accept the powerful's "morality" as morality and found the moral principles of the powerless (as they thought, the only morality) suppressed, here in the "honest versus corrupt" approach the moral principles of the powerless, as pronounced by the ruling power, are regarded as the only right and ethical stand. However, this way of conceptualizing political crimes claims that the powerful only simulates virtue or goodness; it pretends morality, but in fact it does not live up to the demands of the moral standards prescribed for the larger society. In other words, here the apparent promiscuity of the powerful (that is the ruling social-political power) demonstrates a double standard. While it prides itself on declaring moral virtues and ethical demands which should rule in the society, the power itself does not follow them. As a result, the political criminal actually does not reject the stated ethical principles of the ruling power. Rather, he shares and agrees with them, but he commits a political crime to help this morality to a victory that should include the moral behavior of all in the society, even those in power.

Thus, in this conception, the target of political crimes is not the ruling social-political power's prescriptive morality, but, rather, the power's immoral behavior, which deviates from the morality it prescribes for others. The political criminal revolts against the fact that the ruling power does not apply the otherwise "right" morality to itself.

Perhaps it was Louis Proal who spoke out most eloquently and violently against this moral abuse of the ruling power. In contrasting the honest and the corrupt in *Political Crime*, he introduced his idea of who should be regarded as a political criminal.[18] He likes to think of governing as if it were a noble and important art, but his historical examples seem to have convinced him that the rule of power "has been disfigured by a great number of false maxims" that made governing the art of "lying and deceiving," "proscribing and despoiling," all under the cloak of legality. "Humanity has had for its governors," he cried out bitterly, "slaughterers, fanatics, robbers, false coiners, bankrupts, madmen," men who have been corrupt, and men who have sown corruption.[19] His outburst against these "governors" indicates what he thinks the

[18] Proal, *op. cit.*
[19] *Ibid.,* p. xiii.

motivation of the political criminal is. Also, he seems to judge the governors as more socially dangerous than the political criminal, and criminals in general, since, as he suggested, while ordinary criminals kill or rob only a few individuals, the powerful political malefactors have countless victims; moreover they ruin entire nations.

Proal, in entertaining the issue of the demoralizing effect of political power from the early tyrants to the end of the nineteenth century (what a pity that he could not go on to our time!) noted some examples which have shown "that it is possible to be a great king, a great Minister, a great citizen, and at the same time an honest man." [20] Yet, he contended, it was not Machiavelli who invented Machiavellism; all he did was to relate what he saw being done by the politicians, actually by politicians of all times, and this is nothing less than to lie and to become shifty and violent. It is rare for the ruling power, he states, not to corrupt virtues.[21]

Proal, in fact, accuses with crimes (whatever "crime" may mean) both sides in the social structure, the powerful as well as the powerless. Not only "kings, emperors, aristocracies, democracies, republics, all governments have resorted to murder out of political considerations . . . from love of power." [22] Political assassinations, tyrannicides, regicides, mob riots, revolutions, and other acts, usually qualified as political crimes, also often occur as reactions to the governing power's immorality. Proal has postulated a broadened view of political criminals. Included in his definition are politicians who hypocritically act against political rivals, exploit ordinary people through

[20] *Ibid.*, p. 341.
[21] *Ibid.*, p. 2
[22] *Ibid.*, pp. 28–29.

pretended morality, commit evil deeds in the course of elections, use the law as an instrument of injustice to confiscate and rob, use demagoguery to promote agitations and to intimidate, and engage in other similar political activities. But, also, or maybe first of all, Proal includes among his political criminals those nonpoliticians who would agree with the "officially" prescribed morality yet who do not stand up against the "political crimes" of the politicians.

Proal attacks even the historians who habitually admire success without taking the pains to inquire into the corrupt morality of those who appear successful. "They should," he said, "keep a little of the admiration they lavish upon conquerors for the upright men." [23] Although his saddening verdict that the whole society suffers from a moral disease and that, led by the dishonesty of the politicians, so many in the society learn fraud and violence (originally Seneca's proposition), his sympathetic sentiments recognizably turned to those criminals whose law violations were a struggle against corrupt politics. His proposition, based on a natural morality, sees the innocently guilty political criminals victimized by the guilty law-abiding corrupters. Indeed, his stance is not much different from that of Havelock Ellis, who called the political criminals victims of an "attempt by a more or less despotic government to preserve its own stability." [24]

Another of the pioneering "Holy Three of Criminology," Enrico Ferri, whose philosophical orientation might be sensed from his contention that Marx complemented Darwin and Spencer, also claimed in *Criminal*

[23] *Ibid.,* p. 355
[24] Havelock Ellis, *The Criminal* (5th ed., New York, n.d.; preface to 4th ed. dated 1910), p. 1.

Sociology [25] that respect for the law does not develop as a result of police activities and jails, but would spread among people as a result of examples given "by persons in high places and by the authorities themselves." [26] He shared the precept of Gaetano Filangieri, who preceded him by a century, and who believed that disparity in rights precipitates political crimes and that when the citizen is no longer protected by "the sword of justice," he may turn to assassinations.[27] Ferri argued with Napoleone Colajanni who, in his typology, accepted political crime as an independent category and contended against him that many political offenders are "really honest and normal men," [28] not to be confused with ordinary lawbreakers. He called them "evolutive" or "politico-social" criminals,[29] who tend "in a more or less illusory way to hasten the future phases of politico-social life"; [30] and here Ferri not only contrasts the honest with the corrupt, but also leans toward a stance that Bonger took somewhat more clearly.

Observation in our time, primarily on the American scene, of the series of revolutionary acts, popularly called acts and actions against "the Establishment," indeed does not make it clear whether the actors should be classified among Ferri's "evolutives," who take a stand against the existing power structure in order to hasten the historically unavoidable transformation of the society as essentially

---

[25] Enrico Ferri, *Criminal Sociology* (New York, 1967).
[26] *Ibid.*, p. 265.
[27] Gaetano Filangieri, *La Science de la législation* (Paris, 1788) (original in Italian, *Scienza della legislazione*).
[28] Napoleone Colajanni, *Sociologia criminale* (Catania, 1889), vol. 1, p. 352.
[29] Ferri, *op. cit.*, p. 163.
[30] *Ibid.*, p. 335.

proposed by orthodox Marxism, or among the Bongerian class of anarchists who neglect or do not even know the theoretical bases of social change, or among Proal's "honests" who rebel against dishonesty and the corruption of morality and act for the purity of societal institutions.

Although antiwar protests, student activism, college and university confrontations, black militancy, racial attitudes of the whites, so-called police riots, and other acts and action programs, and the accompanying violence, are usually regarded as political in character, they are generally considered "an outgrowth of social, economic, and political conditions," and the violence is usually seen as arising "out of an interaction between protesters and the reaction of authorities." [31] Yet the generalized references to pressing social and economic conditions, the grievances spelled out primarily against the given arrangements of the authority, and the complaints against the "overreaction" of those in charge of maintaining law and order do not make it clear—either on the part of the actors or their interpreters—how and where the attackers of "the Establishment" should be classified.

One of the reasons for this lack of clarity is that even the term "Establishment" has remained beyond explanation. "Establishments" have been opposed or assaulted regardless of whether they represent the whole societal structure or just one of its relatively insignificant segments or institutions. The "political criminals" of our time do not seem to be selective in their understanding of the theory of social change, nor do they impress one

---

[31] Jerome H. Skolnick, *The Politics of Protest*, Task Force Report, vol. 3, "Violent Aspects of Protest and Confrontation," a Staff Report to the National Commission on the Causes and Prevention of Violence, published under the authority of the Commission (Washington, D.C., 1969), p. 3.

with the ability to plan on a magnificent scale. Another of the possibly many reasons for the lack of a clear profile is the almost total neglect (on the part of the actors as well as their interpreters) of the analysis of the problem of morality. which seems to indicate that our contemporary sociologists are not inclined to entertain this question, nor are our lawyers, who are supposed to supply the roots of understanding. In view of this, their "problems of definition"[32] are not really surprising. Clearly, by avoiding the struggle with the problem of morality, the most crucial issue of political criminality, the subject matter cannot cooperate with the evaluation except at the risk of drastic oversimplifications.

Although in the late sixties much research was done on our contemporary "political crimes," beneath the investigators' penetrating gaze no true portrait has begun to take shape. Because these research results paint the picture without involving the problems of morality, it is still only a sketch, its outlines remain necessarily indistinct, and the interpretations appear to be close to an optical illusion. These modern analyses do not seem to offer much more than Lombroso offered in his list of "causes of political crimes"[33] where he included places of convergence, density of population, race relations, arrangements of the government, predominance of one of the social classes, parties and divisions among people, imitations of political law violations and epidemics in a mob, historic traditions, spreading the idea of ideals,

[32] *Ibid.*, pp. 3–6. See also the endless flow of writings on violence from the mid-sixties.

[33] Cesare Lombroso, *Crime: Its Causes and Remedies*, trans. Henry P. Horton (Boston, 1918), pp. 226–244, based on the French version with the help of Kurella's and Jentsch's German translation of Lombroso's *L'uomo delinquente* (Milan, 1876).

inappropriate political reforms, religious reactions, economic influences and crises, aggravated taxes, wars, and other factors. He also mentioned the revolutionary spirit of the "genius" and orography (the study of mountains), but our moderns perhaps have not found a genius among those who have acted against the "Establishment," and perhaps they investigated only the plains or could not recognize the effect of physical environment on crime. But then, Lombroso was interested in the political criminal rather than in political crime.

The Normal and the Abnormal

Perhaps the most challenging question for those who venture to try to conceptualize political crime through the political criminal has always been the problem of the state of mind of the offender and his emotional balance. Lombroso, characteristically, was among the first who paid intense attention not only to the criminal act, but also to the criminal man, and his typology dealt with political criminals rather than with political lawbreakings. He listed political criminals as a subgroup in his class of "criminals by passion" (actually the only subgroup under this heading) and contended that, whatever is true for the passionate criminal, "much the same may be said of the political criminal." [34] Lombroso suggested that criminals by passion can be characterized by a high degree of affectability which, under stress in unusual circumstances, develops a passion that leads to crimes with violence. While not all criminals by passion are political criminals,

[34] *Ibid.*, pp. 412–414.

all political criminals are criminals by passion. Lombroso believed in the passion of the political criminals so strongly that he charged the passionless political criminals with insanity, who "need the hospital more than the scaffold," and actually proposed their deportation.

Lombroso did not contend that political criminals are "born criminals," and he recommended their removal "from the governmental and social environment" because they proved their inability to adapt themselves to other people's accepted power structure. Since he thought that there are political criminals who are "lunatics" or "unbalanced individuals," [35] and that almost all anarchists are "insane," [36] he leaned significantly toward relating some political crimes to mentally or emotionally abnormal individuals and most of them to highly emotional (passionate) persons.

His fancy, as happened with Ferri's notion of "social danger," has become a reality in our time when, perhaps not exactly in the Lombrosian sense, the Soviet system established mental clinics for political prisoners.[37] Since this "penal substitute" (another idea of Enrico Ferri) has been misunderstood in many quarters, in October 1971 the Soviet newspaper *Izvestia* denounced the allegation that healthy people were being sent to mental asylums. "In reality," *Izvestia* claimed, these persons are those "who have committed socially dangerous acts in a state of derangement or who have become mentally ill during in-

[35] Gina Lombroso-Ferrero, *Criminal Man: According to the Classification of Cesare Lombroso* (repr. Montclair, N.J., 1972), p. 298.

[36] *Ibid.,* p. 305.

[37] "Mental Clinics for Political Prisoners," *The Manchester Guardian Weekly,* vol. 104, no. 14 (Apr. 3, 1971), p. 5.

vestigation, trial, or after sentence." [38] Lombroso's contention, however, has not been shared by many who have tackled the concept of the political criminal, for example Havelock Ellis, and who have clearly distinguished political criminals from criminals with passion.[39]

Perhaps it is a coincidence, but the American arena of political criminals also seems to support, at least in its general orientation, the Lombrosian views and the Soviet experiences. In the analysis of "deadly attacks upon public office-holders in the United States" (a list of attacked persons in nine printed pages), which is part of a report to the National Commission on the Causes and Prevention of Violence,[40] there were "problems of definition," and the compilers did not seem to be sure how to categorize attempts by mentally disturbed persons, "such as the typical attacker" of a President of the United States. Mainly because a psychiatrist contributor to the commission's work suggested that, with the possible exception of the attack upon President Harry S. Truman, "there have been no political assassination attempts" directed at the heads of the United States; "the attacks are viewed as products of mental illness with no direct political content." [41]

Although this report admitted the arguable nature of this stance, it maintained that there are pertinent similarities in the personal characteristics of the perpetrators, among them that all the offenders have been mentally

[38] Quoted by *Le Monde*, no. 143, Jan. 15, 1972.
[39] Ellis, *op. cit.*, p. 2.
[40] James F. Kirkham, Sheldon G. Levy, and William J. Crotty, *Assassination and Political Violence*, Task Force Report, vol. 8, a Staff Report to the National Commission on the Causes and Prevention of Violence, published under the authority of the Commission (Washington, D.C., October 1969).
[41] *Ibid.*, pp. 1–2.

disturbed persons with an absence or disruption of the normal family relationship between parent and child.[42] The explanation of the "politicization of the disordered mind" in this report largely disregards the moral prescriptives as they are reflected in the general emotional attitudes of the members of the society. Instead, it speaks quite strongly, in orthodox Freudian terms, hinting at the offenders' unconscious need to commit political crimes.

Maurice Parmelee, in a somewhat similar vein, suggested that insanity, of one kind or another, and other forms of mental morbidity more or less prevail among political criminals. He found only small difference between the pathological and emotional types and observed that "rational" political offenders are "by far the least numerous." [43] Actually, Parmelee placed the criminals by passion in the class of "occasional criminals," and all criminals who commit their crimes under the influence of a distinct psychosis, called by him "psychopathic criminals," came in an independent category.[44] In his view, the "evolutive and political criminals" constitute a special type, in spite of their abnormal state of mind. Following Ferri's thinking and terminology, Parmelee called them "evolutive" criminals because they contribute to social progress (as opposed to his "involutive" ordinary antisocial offenders).

In considering the traits of political criminals, Parmelee divides them into three principal types: the pathologicals, the emotionals, and the rationals. He also contends that "according to political and social conditions,

[42] *Ibid.,* p. 62.
[43] Maurice Parmelee, *Criminology* (New York, 1918), pp. 462–464.
[44] *Ibid.,* pp. 198–201.

anyone may become a criminal" of a political nature.[45] Among the pathologicals he includes those who assassinate monarchs or who kill persons in authority or prominence. Among American political criminals Parmelee would have listed the assassinator of President John F. Kennedy as well as the murderer of Martin Luther King. He catalogs here also those who do such things as throw bombs, explode mines, or kill innocent people in public places.

The emotional type, in Parmelee's categorization, occupies the predominant place with the highest frequency. He proposes that some of them are "sympathetic" since their emotions give rise to compassion for human misfortunes and a desire to ameliorate them. However, Parmelee cautions, anarchists and egoistic, thus unsocial, criminals can also be found among the emotional political offenders. Parmelee downrates the rationals because those whose reasoning faculty is highly developed are deliberate in their conduct and therefore not likely to try to bring about social changes by means of violence except as a last resort.[46] In view of this, Parmelee recommends special tribunals and distinguishing penal consequences for political criminals, for at present there is "a lamentable failure" to make any distinction.[47]

To think of political criminals in terms of "abnormality" or some kind of mental derangement appears reasonable only to those who forget the pluralistic nature of morality and the inadequacies of the socialization processes. The ruling social-political power, understandably, believes in the goodness and rightness of its own pro-

[45] *Ibid.*, p. 461.
[46] *Ibid.*, p. 465.
[47] *Ibid.*, p. 468.

138

claimed and prescribed moral principles. But in the false assumption that all members of the society are well socialized and thus can and do understand the "command" of morality, the sovereign cannot believe that anybody with a sane mind would rebel against his moral tenets. Everything is so good and promising in the society, so the ruling power's and the well-socialized people's argument runs, that only mentally abnormal individuals could oppose it and only pathologically minded persons would commit political crimes. And the traumatic twist in this logic is that it *may be true;* the political criminal just cannot see it so. It may indeed be a "good" society, at least to the extent of the power's and the well-socialized people's belief. The power is convinced that its rule is good for the society, and those who are well socialized (that is, those who have accepted the prescribed morality in the course of their socialization) are happy with the given kind of rule and they think of their society as a good one. But those who do not accept these moral principles (*because* their socialization to this morality has been inadequate), and *therefore* do not feel happy with the morality that guides their society, are not necessarily mentally sick.

Since the political criminal is not taught through rewards and punishments to approve fully the moral prescriptives and commands of the sovereign, he is unable to enjoy or desire them; moreover, his desires belong to a world other than the one he inhabits under the rule of the given social-political power. His perception of the reality of himself and the surrounding social environment is faulty—meaning by "reality" the mode of existence that ought to be socialized into him. He does not, and cannot, understand the principles of the prescribed morality and the reasons for the sovereign's commands. He was not made a model man, and he could not develop those competencies which would have been necessary for coping with the personal and societal problems of a group life as designed by the ruling power.

His inadequately socialized being perceives an unreal world—meaning by "unreality" only a partial acceptance or even total refusal of the mode of existence as expected by his sovereign power and, consequently, a partially or totally different morality and social design. His misunderstanding or nonunderstanding of the moral commands allows him to envisage the possibility of criticizing this world and the way of life as irrational or immoral or both, on the assumption that he, as a critic, recognizes moral principles and societal designs which other critics could have recognized but did not. He does not recognize that these others have been differently or "better" socialized. The political criminal sees no reason for believing that man's true happiness and perfection depend on understanding the place the sovereign assigned to him in this globe. He does not suffer any kind of mental disorder; he is just an inadequately socialized explorer of a vision—a vision that would not emerge if he were adequately socialized.

However, because the political criminal lives in a world that is not real to him he cannot avoid confronting stresses, fears, conflicts, frustrations, anxieties, and pressures—all resulting in emotions, mistaken by some observers as symptoms of some kind of mental derangement. Granted, since "psychologists have not so far done much to illuminate" the obscurity of the nature of emotions,[48] such a mistake is understandable, but it may have fatal consequences.

[48] Jeffrey A. Gray, *The Psychology of Fear and Stress* (New York, 1971), p. 9.

Although severe mental disorders involve loss of contact with reality, with detachment from the real world, often characterized by delusions and hallucinations frequently related even to sensory perceptions, this type of psychosis is usually not confined only to the interpretation of moral issues and social designs, and it can be distinguished from living in another "unreal" world, which is the product of misunderstanding or nonunderstanding of the morality and commands of the sovereign.

Psychotic symptoms may originate from psychological disorders or organic brain pathology, or from the interaction of both, and they manifest a marked personality decompensation.[49] As opposed to an emotional state of mind, they do not give to the patient an insight into the morbid nature of his behavior or offer a possible power to regulate his conduct. Emotion, however, is a conscious experience, without the characteristics of any mental disease. The political criminal's contact with what the ruling power and the well-socialized people call reality appears to *them* weaker, and he lacks insight into *their* moral issues. He has no mental difficulties in registering the state of his social environment, but in the absence of learning its meaning he is a deviant perceiver and an alien in his own world. This is why he reacts to the "reinforcing events" of rewards and punishments (or removal of a punishment or failure of an expected reward) with "emotions," [50] and this is why he has different moral principles.

Lombroso appears to be correct in calling attention to the role of emotions in political criminality, save that

[49] James C. Coleman, *Abnormal Psychology and Modern Life* (3d ed., Chicago, 1964), pp. 262–263.
[50] Gray, *op. cit.*, p. 9.

he qualifies these emotions with pathological features. Emotions aroused in the political criminal because of the conflict between his inadequately socialized world and the well-socialized world do not seem to justify branding him as pathological. Rather, these emotions may make him accuse the society that disturbed him. Because he missed those rewards and punishments which could have taught him to accept the sovereign's moral commands, his growth was not blocked toward desiring moral principles and social designs other than those prescribed and which prevail in his actual society.

This would be more understandable if ethics and aesthetics were treated in the same fashion from the psychological point of view. Eysenck uses the example of judgments in the field of art, where some evaluations are not of an aesthetic nature but are based on what he calls cultural determinants. He states that "the monetary value of the picture, its fame, the fact that it is exhibited by the Royal Academy, knowledge of the position of the painter in the hierarchy of his colleagues"—all these and other considerations determine what people say when asked "Do you like this picture?" [51] But what about those people who have not been socialized to a social design where monetary value, reputation, and popularity in one's reference group are decisive factors in expressing likes or dislikes? Should they be stigmatized with pathological qualities in case they ignore (because they do not know) the importance of these moral prescriptives in forming an aesthetic judgment and, thus, express a different evaluation? And would it be surprising, when observing their emotions in criticizing this "morality" in aesthetics that,

---

[51] H. J. Eysenck, *Sense and Nonsense in Psychology* (Harmondsworth, England, 1957), p. 321.

since they are not socialized to it, they cannot understand?

To live in an "unreal" world within the boundaries of a "real" world unavoidably develops conflicts which generate fears, angers, anxieties, and other emotions that accompany not only the psychic pain in this discomforting social situation, but also the actions and efforts to remove it and replace it with another that promises more comfort. In this unreal world the political criminal becomes emotional because he is pressured by the sovereign to accept the prescribed morality that he does not understand and that, he feels, may demoralize him.

"Morality" and "immorality" are set here against one another, meaning concepts as they appear on each side of the conflict. Emotion does play a significant part in the moral life of the individual, mainly if his mind is barraged by ideologized antagonism that alarms him. His image of a better morality and a happier world (that he envisions because he lacks understanding of the power's prescribed moral issues and social design) leads him to sympathism and eventual acting out, which in turn lead him to accompanying emotional reactions.

Lombroso's and his contemporaries' idea about the emotional morality or passion of political criminals is just one of the many examples that show that our modern sociologists and criminologists do not give new answers to old questions and do not propose questions never asked before: The political offender, in his stressful social situation, is entitled to have emotions. His emotions are a deceptively natural phenomenon that may affect the lucidity of his thoughts, yet they do not make him a candidate for a mental hospital.

5

The Convictional Criminal

The Tragic Dilemma of the Political Criminal

In an attempt to reconcile the different under-standings of the concept of the political criminal, taking into account mainly those which call attention to his passion and strong feelings for society, the term *convictional criminal* is here proposed.[1] The political criminal is "con-

---

[1] In English first proposed by Stephen Schafer, "Juvenile Delinquents in 'Convictional Crime,'" *International Annals of Criminology*, 1 (Paris, 1963), pp. 45–51. The probable original German term *"Der Überzeugungsverbrecher,"* appeared perhaps first in a "Draft of a General German Criminal Code" (*Entwurf eines Allgemeinen Deutschen Strafgesetzbuches*) to which Gustav Radbruch responded in his "Der Überzeugungsverbrecher" (44 *Zeitschrift für die gesamte Strafrechtswissenschaft*, 1924, pp. 36–37) where he opposed the ordinary punishment and claimed penal consequences with special purpose for political criminals, because, as he suggested, they cannot be "bettered." Radbruch discussed this contention first in *Einführung* (4th ed., 1919, pp. 93ff). The German term has been used also in the Remarks (*Bemerkungen*) to the mentioned Draft Code, submitted in 1929 to the German Ministry of Justice. In Italian *delinquente per convinzione*, see in

vinced" about the truth and justification of his own beliefs, which, in their ultimate analysis, are the products of his defective perception of the moral commands of the sovereign power.

This element of "conviction" may serve as a distinguishing factor in discriminating the political criminal from the ordinary offender. It is a settled belief, essentially a deep-seated consideration in the political criminal's conscience that makes him feel that he has a rendezvous with destiny, that he is a David striking at a Goliath of injustice on a world scale, capable of imposing an order on the chaos of reality.

Convictional criminals may be distinguished from conventional criminals, and also from "pseudoconvictional" criminals, who just look like the genuine political criminals but in fact do not really differ from the prosaic violators of law. If a prophet can be described as a man who sees the political society as complex as it is and the moral issue as simple as it is, then the political criminal might be justified in perceiving himself as a prophet or even possibly a saint. After all he has a passion for the impossible that he believes is possible. As he perceives the world, man's function is not to stabilize, but to direct energies and inspire actions. To illustrate the proposed term, in the example of Louis Proal, while it is not "lawful to kill in order to secure the triumph of a cause," [2] the political criminal may be "convinced" of the correctness of such a statement, yet he disregards the law.

By contrast with the convictional criminal, the conventional offender almost always acts to fulfill his ego or personal interest, and his acts often lack an overarching

---

Stephen Schafer, "Il Delinquente Politico," *Quaderni di Criminologia Clinica*, 1 (March 1972), pp. 42–61.

[2] Louis Proal, *Political Crime* (New York, 1898), p. 50.

coherence.[3] Although the occasional or casual criminal may steal a loaf of bread when hungry, shoplift a diamond ring if overcome by desire, or kill another out of jealousy, it is *his* hunger, *his* desire, or *his* kind of emotion against his rival, and he must be stimulated by personal need, wish, or agitation of mind. When the professional criminal burgles a bank, he acts for *his* personal gain; and when the drug addict forges a medical prescription, he does so to satisfy *his* personal addiction to narcotics. Even if the mentally sick person is led to homicide by his delusions or hallucinations, these false impressions are symptoms of *his* mental illness.

The convictional criminal, on the other hand, has an altruistic-communal motivation rather than an egoistic drive. It is not simply altruistic, however, inasmuch as his regard for others as a principle of his action is not confined to the personal interests of specified individuals. Homicide as revenge for another person, for example, or the stealing of bread to feed members of one's family are not convictional crimes, although committed for others' sake. The convictional criminal's altruism is a nonpersonal communal experience, aiming at some sort of moral or social change—not necessarily for a change of the moral or social total, since it may be aimed only at a segment of the whole or even at a single moral or social issue related to governmental, societal, ethical, or religious ideals which affect communal interests. Lombroso and Laschi suggested that the French Revolution was not a struggle against an individual king or even a dynasty, but against the institutions of monarchy and feudalism, and Lutheranism was not a revolt against the pope, but against the corruption that had invaded the Roman Catholic Church.

[3] See Stephen Schafer and Richard D. Knudten, Juvenile Delinquency: An Introduction (New York, 1970), pp. 165–168.

The convictional law violator's altruism is seen as communal not only because it may come into conflict with the prevailing morality and social design of the ruling power structure, but also because his violation of the law intends to make moral and societal ideals legitimate through crime, and his deviance is for the purpose of achieving progress in his society. The legendary hero who robbed the rich to give money to the poor, the suffragette who agitated for women's votes in order to force changes in the law, members of the Resistance who injured others to hamper the invader, the counterrevolutionary who killed to crush an opposing ideology, for example, represented altruistic-communal ideas and ideals. They committed crimes because they were convinced about the justice of their beliefs and because crime appeared to them as the route, maybe the only route, to effect unselfish concern for the welfare of a social group. The crime of the convictional criminal, from origin to completion, appeals to him in the panorama of his altruistic-communal vision.

Through the telescope of his conviction, the distant object of his ideal is seen to loom large, giving his crime secondary importance. However, this is not owing to his passion, since at least in the pure concept the convictional criminal is not "passionate," except when the term "passion" is used in its old meaning, which identified it with emotions in general.[4] The convictional criminal does not discount the implications of crime and punishment, but this is not because some passionate outburst clouds his consideration. He takes his stand for his altruistic-communal belief *frigido pacatoque animo,* with "cool and

---

[4] "Passion" was the term used by older writers when referring to emotions in general, but it is now reserved for violent emotional outbreaks. See James Drever, *A Dictionary of Psychology* (Harmondsworth, England, 1952), p. 199.

peaceful mind." In fact, this is why he is able to "convince" himself. If his conviction appears colored with emotions, this can be attributed not only to his conflict and to the fact that no moral decision making is possible without some sort of emotional involvement, but also to a dilemma he has to solve before turning to crime.

A genuine convictional criminal cannot escape from this dilemma, and he inevitably faces a catastrophic internal clash between two antagonistic beliefs, which creates a major psychic and ethical strain, for it represents a nearly insoluble and tragic contradiction between moral and social demands. One is his loyalty to the general principles of law and order and condemnation of crime; the other is his conviction concerning the justice of his cause and his assumption that only crime can promote it.

Although the convictional criminal struggles to reconcile the two loyalties and feels tormented by the apparent contrast between the two responsibilities, he commits his crime out of a sense of convinced obligation for his own morality. Because of the force of his conviction, he cannot refrain from violation of law, even at the sacrifice of his life or freedom and his loyalty to law and order, in which otherwise he believes. Gripped by an obsession that results from his original conflict, he regains energy as his original impotence, caused by the pressure of the misunderstood or nonunderstood moral command, gives way to an emotional conviction that ultimately has no law: Crime appears to him the only key to the door of his cause.

Bar-Kokhba, the "son of a star," for example, believed in obedience, but he became the hero of the last Jewish revolt against Imperial Rome. The legendary Robin Hood may have disapproved of robbery, but he committed many thefts to benefit the poor. One should not forget that Jean-

Jacques Rousseau never ceased to believe in God, despite his great respect for Socratic teaching. A member of the Second World War Resistance, again for example, may have condemned violence, yet his own conviction over-shadowed any sense of repugnance and induced him to engage in violent crimes in an effort to expel the invader from his fatherland. The counterrevolutionary knew that homicide is a capital crime, yet he killed for the good of his nation.

The political criminal's crime often mirrors the hopes of all those common people who are likewise inadequately socialized to the moral command, but who somehow do not reach the degree of inner conflict that can lead to the action-prompting emotional dilemma. The political crim-inal is one of these, but through his forceful conflict and dilemma he becomes a kind of creator, fulfilled only when he creates, even at the price of crime, and unfulfilled when he passively receives or drifts with the moral current. He is so convinced that, as Lewis Coser remarked, "one may argue with an innovator, but hardly with a criminal"; [5] the highly emphasized dysfunction of deviance, as seen in the literature of social control, he claims, traditionally neglects the analysis of its function. But this functional deviance may be observed in the conflict-directed action of the con-victional criminal.

The Instrumentality of the Convictional Crime

The high pressure of his ideal causes the convic-tional criminal to commit crime. Since, however, he views

[5] Lewis A. Coser, "Some Functions of Deviant Behavior and Normative Flexibility," *The American Journal of Sociology,* 68, no. 2 (September 1962), p. 178.

crime as disobedience or disloyalty to the laws of his society and as an evil deed against law and order, but not as an expression of immorality, his internal conflict does not result from fear of penal consequences.

Although he may show signs of anxiety and agitation, they are not directly associated with the crime itself. Crime is not his main purpose but only an act that intervenes between his convictional decision and his ultimate ideal which may lead eventually to other similar crimes and, at the end, to the successful implementation of his cause. Consequently, his violation of the law is not a self-contained behavior, but an "instrumental crime" for moral ideological purposes. The legendary hero's goal, for example, was not robbery, but aid to the poor. The violence of the Resistance member was only a tool to crush the invader. Nevertheless, the commission of crime puts a temporary end to the convictional criminal's anxiety. Although he may not yet have realized his ideal, he sees his crime as a step toward the end accomplishment. His tragic dilemma is resolved and his psychic balance is restored through the force of his conviction that guided him to the commission of the criminal act. His intellectual response to his own crime therefore proceeds in a specfic direction.

As the ordinary criminal undergoes relatively minimal internal struggle before committing his crime, his anxiety is confined mainly to careful planning, maintenance of security, and accomplishing successful criminal action. The convictional criminal, on the other hand, is often less concerned with the actual mechanics of his crime. Although his excitment may be greater, he seeks a difficult goal that goes well beyond the crime itself. While the conventional criminal is often restless after the crime has been committed, possibly because of pangs of conscience, fear of arrest, and other conditions that may upset his psychic equilibrium, the convictional criminal, his conscience satisfied, is relieved by his crime, and his balance is restored.

Since every breach of secrecy may jeopardize his success and his future, the conventional criminal places great importance upon security. Planning, preparation, and the hiding place of plunder are kept confidential. He does his best to maintain security among his accomplices and, to an extent, even among his victims. Any form of publicity presents a danger to the ordinary criminal. In contrast, the convictional criminal, with his altruistic moral ideology, places less emphasis upon secrecy and even seeks publicity for his cause. He hides and disguises his activities only to promote his further goals. His motivation, his antagonism toward given moral issues, and the propagation of his ultimate aim are communal in character and generally serve his final objective—the promotion of an ideal.

Dramatic publicity is therefore almost a necessity for the convictional criminal in order to make the public understand his actions. He influences others to guilty introspection, he lets them see something they had failed to to see for themselves, and he guides them to this revelation in a fashion that is morally pleasant to them. Jesus made no attempt to defend or conceal himself. By claiming to be the Christ, the King of the Jews, he was automatically committing treason against Rome, and his punishment attracted the attention of millions of followers generation after generation. Tales of the robberies of the legendary hero, the dramatic stories of Resistance members, or the sight of the counterrevolutionaries' reckless deeds, for example, inspired the poor, recruited new fighters, or excited others to participation in an uprising.

Publicity about convictional crimes almost inevitably

leads to further crimes. As the convictional criminal succeeds in disseminating his ideals among the members of his society, the number of convictional crimes tends to increase. His crime may serve as an example to would-be followers. As the convictional crime may even be supported by public opinion, punishment of the offender may fail to deter later convictional crimes. Moreover, punishment may serve only to interest others in the given ideal and to recruit members for other convictional violations of law. As the acts of the legendary hero, for example, stimulated and encouraged others to overcome their inhibitions, they too joined in robbing the rich. As the violent activity of the Resistance inflamed others, they also acted criminally against occupation forces. As the counter-revolutionaries' fight for freedom touched the consciences of fellow citizens, they also followed the path of blood.

Of course, the publicity may be abortive in generating offenses and violence rather than political crimes in the line of the political criminal's morality-oriented lawbreaking. We have seen this in our time when we live in a violent world that is dangerous whatever moral stand one may take. Violence, which is not to be confused with the physical force often employed by the genuine convictional criminal, seems to have become our American way of life. Even in the relatively disciplined England, as reported by the newspapers, at recent Christmastimes one of the suitable presents for children has been a "riot control coloring set" that shows a man with a truncheon hitting another on the ground. The stimulating publicity of the convictional criminal's crime is apt to contribute to an epidemic emergence of violent acts. But in all fairness it must be said that much of this stems from those who selfishly choose which laws and morality they wish to respect and which to ignore, and from those who assert their rights but recognize no obligations, rather than from the altruistic emotions of the political criminal. Muddling the two kinds of violence might be an unforgivable theoretical error.

It is quite an exception that the names of the intellectual leaders of a conspiracy against the English King James I (Robert Catesby, Thomas Winter, Francis Tresham, and others) faded out at the expense of the instant recognition of the name of Guy Fawkes, the only professional hired for the Gunpowder Plot on November 4, 1605, immediately tried and executed four days later opposite the Parliament buildings; but the bonfires and fireworks in November each year do not really remind the British of an ordinary offender. Rather they appear to celebrate the failure of a crime that promoted the rise and domination of their Parliament.

The Pseudoconvictional Criminal

Not all who commit crimes with the apparent motive of promoting the triumph of an altruistic-communal cause are genuine convictional criminals. Not all contemplate the justice of an ideal, and not all are tormented by the tragic dilemma of loyalties, which is actually an unconditional qualification for entering the ranks of true political criminals. "The activist is tempted by opportunism, the urge to adjust his arguments to meet every change in political fortune," and "the scientist faces the danger of losing touch with common political concerns." [6] The multitude of pseudoconvictional criminals, and their

[6] "The Laws behind Disorder," *The Times Literary Supplement* (London), no. 3603, Mar. 19, 1971, p. 309.

skill in hiding their opportunist criminal identity, poses the greatest problem for identification of the true political criminal. If a test were devised for the detection of the pseudoconvictional criminal, and for measuring the functional role of the hypothesis of "conviction," however much discernible hazard would be associated with any such undertaking, it could bring us closer to the concept of the political criminal. It would be indeed a delicate task, since even truly heroic virtues are corroded when they are reduced to being dedicated to mere self-esteem.

Many simply use the convictional ideal as an excuse for their own criminal act. Moved by love or hate, penchant for adventure, psychopathic deviation, justification of avoiding constructive work, or hope for gain, the pseudoconvictional offenders may join forces with the true convictional criminal and demonstrate the criminality and "immorality of political maxims." [7] Some friends of the legendary hero, for example, joined him because of their thirst for adventure. Some followers of the Resistance took the opportunity to satisfy their criminal inclinations. Some participants in counterrevolution sought future or even immediate rewards. These were individuals attracted to convictional law violations by egoistic motives. Their targets were an individualistic goal through crime, not the service of an ideal, and an advantage for themselves rather than for others.

Any aggressive idealistic movement, regardless of the prevailing moral and social system, is likely to have both convictional and pseudoconvictional participants. Pseudoconvictional criminals happen to exist even in democracies where government by the consent of the governed is often said to be one of the essentials of the social design,

[7] Proal, *op. cit.*, pp. 1–23.

but where the modern usage of the term "consent" has become so vague and fluid that it enables the pseudoconvictional law violators to employ it to justify for the masses any of their egoistic actions against almost any regime. Often their message seems not so much untimely as exaggerated to the point of pointlessness, and yet it incites others to crimes for their own benefit.

While the genuine convictional political criminal has a moral base, though opposing the ruling power's moral prescriptions, the pseudoconvictional offender represents the diabolic corruption of any honorable dispute over the pluralistic nature of moral principles. He is often supported by the bulk of inadequately socialized and frustrated ordinary men, who in each generation and each class need legends and seem condemned to a perpetual search for reassuring heroes, albeit what these heroes have in common is the abnegation of ultimate responsibility.

The pseudoconvictional criminal has a high-pitched declamation like the "Hear me, Wotan, hear me," that Erda sings in *Das Rheingold* as she rises to the surface of the earth to deliver her dire warning of disasters to come. One of the persistent paradoxes of these heroes' persuasive radicalism is their avoidance of substantive issues and concrete material by taking refuge either in extreme skepticism or in religious certainty. The pseudoconvictional criminal is dominated by his personal goals. By imitating a genuine convictional criminal he simply takes advantage of the altruistic ideals to steal, rob, or murder or to incite others to do so.

For students of modern politics there are fascinating glimpses of life in the corridors of power struggle. Actually, the pseudoconvictional political criminal is not an invention of our television age, yet his appearance on the scene is on the increase. While we have a decreasing

number of young Robespierres who would resign a judge-
ship rather than inflict the death penalty, there are many
who aspire to the chair of judge, even at the price of in-
flicting capital punishment. Their topics are beset by
clichés and gloomy truisms, they try to loosen the bonds
that bind society, they try to make us surrender to their
assaults on reason, logic, propriety, and even the language
—however, not for a new or different morality that would
be born from the misunderstanding or nonunderstanding
of the ruling power's moral principles, but only for their
own personal advantage.

Thus, they appear at a respectability level even lower
than that of a pickpocket or bankrobber, who at least hon-
estly admits his egoistic goals. Also, the pseudoconvictional offender is more dangerous than any other criminal
type, more perilous than the thief, the burglar, or the rap-
ist, not only because he may be able to make innocent
people criminals, but because he victimizes the collec-
tivity. He is even more dangerous than the true political
criminal because he makes himself a public figure of his
private world and proposes a profound transformation of
morality without making known his parasite aspirations.
This man, stripped of his mask, is not very different from
the ordinary lawbreaker, perhaps his major distinguishing feature is that, contrary to the genuine convictional
criminal and to the simple offenders, he is closer to understanding the sovereign's moral command, yet he violates it for his own personal greed.

The lessons of history about allowing the pseudoconvictional offender to use others' misguided beliefs to his
own advantage, and about avoiding martyring him by not
punishing his selfish rebellion, are not very hopeful augu-
ries. And the moral and social history of our century indicates that attempts to restore the virginity of the world

may be hopeless. Thus we have to count upon the continuing existence of pseudoconvictional criminals. Life already is becoming dehumanized enough even without their further hastening that process of brutalization by abolishing all kinds of moralities and by destroying all honesties, whatever moral principles they represent. Their increasingly forceful activities may smother the emergence of the genuine convictional criminal.

This challenging future prospect for the true political criminal may continue into the next three decades, going over to the next century, if mankind can survive that long. Centuries-old clichés may continue to be used as an escape from asking serious questions; faith in the political criminal may fatally falter in action; action may falsify the faith; and the concept of the genuine convictional criminal may finally disappear as it gives place to the only alternative: the operation of the pseudoconvictional criminal.

However, despite our global degradation, human imbalance, and decaying conditions, still perhaps we humans are neither sleepwalkers nor sheep. We may be learning just in time.

Selected Bibliography

The problem of morals, laws, crimes, and social realities, from the earliest analyses through Mill and Stephen to contemporary thinkers, has a vast literature. Works listed here in this Selected Bibliography refer only to those which particularly influenced the author.

AHERN, M. B.: *The Problem of Evil*, London, 1971.

ALIMENA, B.: *Naturalismo critico e diritto penale*, Roma, 1892.

ANCEL, MARC: "Social Defence," *Law Quarterly Review*, 1962.

ANGYAL, PÁL: *A magyar büntetöjog tankönyve*, Budapest, 1920.

ASCHAFFENBURG, GUSTAV: *Das Verbrechen und seine Bekämpfung*, Heidelberg, 1903.

AUSTIN, JOHN: *Lectures on Jurisprudence or the Philosophy of Positive Law*, London, 1861.

BAETS, M. DE: *L'école d'anthropologie criminelle*, Gand, 1893.

BAETS, M. DE: *Les influences de la misère sur la criminalité*, Gand, 1895.

BARNSLEY, JOHN H.: *The Social Reality of Ethics*, London, 1972.

BATTAGLIA, BRUNO: *La dinamica del delitto*, Napoli, 1886.

BECCARIA, MARQUIS DE, CESARE BONESANA: *Dei delitti e delle pene*, Haarlem, 1764.

BENN, STANLEY, AND RICHARD S. PETERS: *The Principles of Political Thought*, London and New York, 1965.

BENTHAM, JEREMY: *Principles of Penal Law*, Edinburgh, 1843.

BERGBOHM, KARL: *Jurisprudenz und Rechtsphilosophie*, Leipzig, 1892.

BERMAN, HAROLD J.: *Justice in the U.S.S.R.*, rev. ed., New York, 1963.

BIERLING, RUDOLF ERNST: *Zur Kritik der juristischen Grundbegriffe*, Leipzig, 1877–1893.

BINDING, KARL: *Die erstehung der öffentlichen Strafe in germanisch-deutschem Recht*, Leipzig, 1908.

BOCKELMAN, PAUL: *Studien zum Täterstrafrecht*, Berlin, 1940.

BODENHEIMER, EDGAR: *Jurisprudence: The Philosophy and Method of the Law*, Cambridge, Mass., 1962.

BONGER, WILLEM ADRIAAN: *Criminality and Economic Conditions*, trans. Henry P. Horton, repr. New York, 1967.

BOWERS, PRATIMA: *Consciousness and Freedom*, London, 1971.

BÜRGER-PRINZ, H.: *Motiv und Motivation*, Berlin, 1950.

Campus Unrest, The Report of the President's Commission on Campus Unrest, Washington, D.C., 1970.

CARDOZO, BENJAMIN NATHAN: *The Growth of the Law*, New Haven, Conn., 1924.

CARRARA, FRANCESCO: *Programma*, 6th ed., Torino, 1886.

CASTBERG, FREDE: *Problems of Legal Philosophy*, trans. unknown, Oslo, 1957.

CHRISTIANSEN, KARL O.: "Kriminologie (Grundlagen)," in Rudolf Sieverts (ed.), *Handwörterbuch der Kriminologie*, vol. II, 2d ed., Berlin, 1968.

Civil Disorders, Report of The National Advisory Commission on Civil Disorders, with "Supplemental Studies," Washington, D.C., 1968.

CLINARD, MARSHALL B., AND RICHARD QUINNEY: *Criminal Behavior Systems: A Typology*, New York, 1967.

COHEN, ALBERT K.: "The Sociology of the Deviant Act: Anomie Theory and Beyond," *American Sociological Review*, vol. 1 (1965).

Selected Bibliography

COHEN, MORRIS RAPHAEL: *Reason and Law*, New York, 1961.

COLAJANNI, NAPOLEONE: *Sociologia criminale*, Catania, 1889.

COLEMAN, JAMES C.: *Abnormal Psychology and Modern Life*, 3d ed., Chicago, 1964.

COMTE, ISIDORE AUGUSTE MARIE FRANÇOIS XAVIER: *Système de politique positive, ou traité de sociologie*, 2d ed., Paris, 1890.

CORNE, A.: Les criminels, Paris, 1889.

COSER, LEWIS A.: "Some Functions of Deviant Behavior and Normative Flexibility," *The American Journal of Sociology*, vol. 68, 1962.

CRESSEY, DONALD R.: "Criminological Research and the Definition of Crime," *American Journal of Sociology*, 1951.

CRESSEY, DONALD R.: "Crime," in Robert K. Merton and Robert A. Nisbet (eds.), *Contemporary Social Problems*, 2d ed., New York, 1966.

DAHM, GEORG: "Die Erneuerung der Ehrenstrafe," *Deutsche Juristenzeitung*, 1934.

DAHM, GEORG: *Der Tätertyp im Strafrecht*, Leipzig, 1940.

DEVLIN, PATRICK: *The Enforcement of Morals*, London, 1968.

DIAMOND, A. S.: *Primitive Law*, London, 1935.

DONAGAN, A.: "Mr. Hare and the Conscientious Nazi," *Philosophical Studies*, 1964–1965.

DRÄHMS, AUGUST: *The Criminal: His Personnel and Environment*, New York, 1900.

DRESSER, HORATIO W.: *Ethics in Theory and Application*, New York, 1925.

DROBISCH, M. W.: *Die moralische Statistik und die Willensfreiheit*, Leipzig, 1867.

DUGUIT, LÉON: *L'état, le droit objectif et la loi positive*, Paris, 1901.

DUNNING, WILLIAM ARCHIBALD: *A History of Political Theories from Luther to Montesquieu*, New York, 1902.

DURKHEIM, ÉMILE: *De la division du travail social*, Paris, 1893.

EHRLICH, EUGEN: *The Fundamental Principles of the Sociology of Law*, Cambridge, Mass., 1936.

ELLIS, HAVELOCK: *The Criminal*, 5th ed., New York, n.d.

ELSTER, ALEXANDER, AND HEINRICH LINGEMANN (eds.): *Handwörterbuch der Kriminologie und der anderen strafrechtlichen Hilfswissenschaften*, Berlin and Leipzig, 1933.

EYSENCK, H. J.: *Uses and Abuses of Psychology*, Harmondsworth, England, 1953.

FELDBRUGGE, F. J.: *Soviet Criminal Law: General Part*, Leyden, 1964.

FERRI, ENRICO: *I nuovi orizzonti del diritto e della procedura penale*, Torino, 1881.

FERRI, ENRICO: *La Sociologia criminale*, Torino, 1884.

FERRI, ENRICO: *Criminal Sociology*, trans. Joseph I. Kelly and John Lisle, repr. New York, 1967.

FILANGIERI, GAETANO: *La Science de la législation*, Paris, 1788.

FITZGERALD, P. J.: *Criminal Law and Punishment*, Oxford, 1962.

FLATHMAN, RICHARD E.: *Political Obligation*, New York, 1972.

FLEW, A.: "The Justification of Punishment," *Philosophy*, 1954.

FRANCK, A.: *Philosophie du droit pénal*, Paris, 1864.

FRIEDMANN, WOLFGANG: *Law in a Changing Society*, Baltimore, 1964.

FRIEDRICH, CARL JOACHIM: *The Philosophy of Law in Historical Perspective*, 2d ed., Chicago, 1963.

FULLER, LON L.: *The Morality of Law*, New Haven, Conn., 1964.

GARDINER, P. L.: "On Assenting to a Moral Principle," *Proceedings of the Aristotelian Society*, 1954–1955.

GAREIS, KARL: *Rechtsenzyklopädie und Methodologie*, 2d ed., Stuttgart, 1900.

GAROFALO, RAFFAELE: *Criminology*, trans. Robert Wyness Millar, Boston, 1914.

GARRAUD, E.: *Traité théorique et pratique du droit pénal français*, 3d ed., Paris, 1913.

Selected Bibliography

GELLNER, E. A.: "Ethics and Logic," *Proceedings of the Aristotelian Society*, 1954–1955.

GÉNY, FRANÇOIS: *Méthodes d'interprétation et sources de droit positif*, Paris, 1919.

GEORGE, RICHARD T. DE: *Soviet Ethics and Morality*, Ann Arbor, Mich., 1969.

GINSBERG, MORRIS: *On Justice in Society*, Harmondsworth, England, 1965.

GOLDING, M. P. (ed.): *The Nature of Law: Readings in Legal Philosophy*, New York, 1966.

GOLDSTEIN, ABRAHAM, AND JOSEPH GOLDSTEIN: *Crime, Law and Society*, New York, 1971.

GOLUNSKII, S. A., AND M. S. STROGOVICH: *Teorija gosudarstva i prava*, Moscow, 1940.

GOODMAN, ANTHONY: *The Loyal Conspiracy: The Lords Apellant under Richard II*, London, 1972.

GRAY, J. GLENN: *On Understanding Violence Philosophically and Other Essays*, New York, 1970.

GRAZIA, ALFRED DE: *The Elements of Political Science*, New York, 1965.

GRICE, GEOFFREY RUSSELL: *The Grounds of Moral Judgment*, Cambridge, 1967.

GUERRY, ANDRÉ MICHAEL: *Essai sur la statistique morale*, Paris, 1833.

GUERRY, ANDRÉ MICHAEL: *Statistique morale de l'Angleterre comparée avec la statistique morale de la France*, Paris, 1864.

GURVITCH, GEORGES: *Sociology of Law*, New York, 1942.

HAAG, ERNEST VAN DEN: "Moral Rights and the Law," *The Intercollegiate Review*, vol. 8, 1972.

HÄGERSTRÖM, AXEL ANDERS THEODOR: *Inquiries into the Nature of Law and Morals*, trans. C. D. Broad, Uppsala, 1953.

HALL, JEROME: "From Legal Theory to Integrative Jurisprudence," *Cincinnati Law Review*, vol. 33, 1964.

HANEY, GERHARD: *Sozialistisches Recht und Persönlichkeit*, Berlin, 1967.

THE POLITICAL CRIMINAL

HANON, A.: *De la définition du crime*, Paris, 1893.

HARE, RICHARD MERVYN: *The Language of Morals*, Oxford, 1952.

HARE, RICHARD MERVYN: "Universalizability," *Proceedings of the Aristotelian Society*, 1954–1955.

HARE, RICHARD MERVYN: *Freedom and Reason*, Oxford, 1963.

HARE, RICHARD MERVYN: *Application of Moral Philosophy*, London, 1972.

HART, HERBERT LIONEL ADOLPHUS, "Positivism and the Separation of Law and Morals," *Harvard Law Review*, vol. 71, 1958.

HART, HERBERT LIONEL ADOLPHUS: *The Concept of Law*, Oxford, 1961.

HART, HERBERT LIONEL ADOLPHUS: *Law, Liberty, and Morality*, New York, 1963.

HART, HERBERT LIONEL ADOLPHUS: *Punishment and Responsibility*, Oxford, 1968.

HAZARD, JOHN N.: *The Soviet System of Government*, Chicago, 1964.

HEGEL, GEORG WILHELM: *Encyclopädie der philosophischen Wissenschaften*, Leipzig, 1923.

HOBBES, THOMAS: *Leviathan*, first publ. 1651.

HOEBEL, E. ADAMSON: *The Law of Primitive Man: A Study in Comparative Legal Dynamics*, Cambridge, Mass., 1954.

HOLDSWORTH, W. S.: *A History of English Law*, London, 1903–1909.

HORVÁTH, BARNA: *Angol Jogelmélet*, Budapest, 1943.

IHERING, RUDOLF: *Kampf ums Recht*, Vienna, 1872.

IHERING, RUDOLF: *Geist des römischen Rechts*, Leipzig, 1873.

IHERING, RUDOLF: *Der Zweck im Recht*, Leipzig, 1877–1883.

JANKA, KARL: *Die Strafrechtliche Nothstand*, Vienna, 1878.

JELLINEK, GEORG: *Die Sozialethische Bedeutung von Recht, Unrecht, und Strafe*, Vienna, 1878.

JOLY, HENRY: *Le crime*, Paris, 1888.

KANTOROWITZ, HERMANN: *Die Aufgabe der Soziologie*, Leipzig, 1923.

Selected Bibliography

KANTOROWITZ, HERMANN: *Tat und Schuld*, Zürich, 1933.

KAREVA, M. P., AND G. I. FEDJKIN (eds.): *Teorija gosudarstva i prava*, Moscow, 1955.

KATONÁNÉ, SOLTÉSZ MÁRTA: *Személyiség és jog*, Budapest, 1972.

KELSEN, HANS: *Der juristische und der soziologische Staatsbegriff*, Tübingen, 1922.

KELSEN, HANS: *Allgemeine Staatslehre*, Berlin, 1925.

KELSEN, HANS: "The Pure Theory of Law: Its Methods and Fundamental Concepts," *The Law Quarterly Review*, 1934.

KERIMOV, D. A., A. J. KOROLIEV, AND M. D. SHARGORODSKII: *Obshchaia teorija gosudarstva i prava*, Leningrad, 1961.

KOHLER, JOSEF: *Shakespeare vor dem Forum der Jurisprudenz*, Berlin, 1884.

LAINE, PASCAL: *L'irrévolution*, Paris, 1971.

LAMMASCH, HEINRICH: *Das Recht der Auslieferung wegen politischer Verbrechen*, Vienna, 1884.

LAMMASCH, HEINRICH: *Auslieferungspflicht und Asylrecht*, Leipzig, 1887.

LASKI, HAROLD J.: *Studies in the Problem of Sovereignty*, New Haven, Conn., 1917.

LASKI, HAROLD J.: *Studies in Law and Politics*, London, 1932.

LASKI, HAROLD J.: *The State in Theory and Practice*, London, 1936.

LISZT, FRANZ VON: *Das Verbrechen als Sozialpathologische Erscheinung*, Dresden, 1899.

LLEWELLYN, KARL N.: *Jurisprudence: Realism in Theory and Practice*, New York, 1962.

LLOYD, DENNIS: *The Idea of Law*, Baltimore, 1964.

LLOYD, DENNIS: *Introduction to Jurisprudence*, 2d ed., London, 1969.

LOMBROSO, CESARE: *L'uomo delinquente*, Milano, 1876.

LOMBROSO, CESARE, WITH RODOLFO LASCHI: *Il delitto politico e le rivulozioni*, Torino, 1890.

LOMBROSO, CESARE: *Delitti vecchi e delitti nuovi*, Torino, 1902.

LUNDSTEDT, ANDERS VILHELM: *Legal Thinking Revised: My Own Views on Law*, trans. unknown, Stockholm, 1956.

LUX, H.: *Sozialpolitisches Handbuch*, Berlin, 1892.

MACINTYRE, ALASDAIR: "What Morality Is Not," *Philosophy*, 1957.

MÁDL, FERENC: *A deliktuális felelösség*, Budapest, 1964.

MAESTRO, MARCELLO T.: *Voltaire and Beccaria as Reformers of Criminal Law*, New York, 1942.

MAINE, SIR HENRY SUMNER: *Ancient Law: Its Connection with the Early History of Society and Its Relation to Modern Ideas*, 1861, with Introduction and Notes by Sir Frederick Pollock, London, 1906.

MAKAREWICZ, J.: *Einführung in die Philosophie des Strafrechts auf entwicklungeschichtlicher Grundlage*, Stuttgart, 1906.

MANNHEIM, KARL: *Systematic Sociology: An Introduction to the Study of Society*, J. S. Erös and W. A. C. Stewart (eds.), New York, 1957.

MARTITZ, FR.: *Internationale Rechtshilfe in Strafsachen*, Leipzig, 1888–1897.

MAXWELL, J.: *Le Concept social du crime*, Paris, 1914.

MAYR, GEORG VON: *Moralstatistik mit Einschluss der Kriminalstatistik*, Tübingen, 1917.

MENSHAGIN, V. D., A. A. GERTSENZON, M. M. ISHAIEV, A. A. PIONTOVSKII, AND B. S. UTEVSKII: *Szovjet Büntetöjog*, Budapest, 1951.

MERKEL, ADOLF: *Juristische Encyclopädie*, 7th ed., Leipzig, 1922.

MERTON, ROBERT K.: "Social Structure and Anomie," *American Sociological Review*, 3 (1938): 672–682.

MEZGER, EDMUND: *Strafrecht*, Munich, 1948.

MILLS, C. WRIGHT: *The Power Elite*, New York, 1956.

MOMMSEN, THEODOR: *Römisches Strafrecht*, Leipzig, 1899.

MOMMSEN, THEODOR: *Zum ältesten Strafrecht der Kulturvölker*, Leipzig, 1905.

Selected Bibliography

Moór, Gyula: *Bevezetés a jogfilozófiába*, Budapest, 1922.

Moór, Gyula: *Macht, Recht, Moral*, Szeged, 1922.

Müller-Freinfels, Richard: *Philosophie der Individualität*, Berlin, 1921.

Neumann, Franz: *Behemoth: The Structure and Practice of National Socialism, 1933–1944*, New York, 1963.

Northrop, Filmer Stuart Cuckow: "Ethical Relativism in the Light of Recent Legal Science," *Journal of Philosophy*, 51 (1955), 649–662.

Oettingen, Alexander V.: *Die Moralstatistik in ihrer Bedeutung für eine Sozialethik*, 3d ed., Erlangen, 1882.

Olivecrona, Knut Hans Karl: *Law as Fact*, trans. unknown, Copenhagen and London, 1939.

Oppenheimer, H.: *The Rationale of Punishment*, London, 1913.

Orwell, George: "The Freedom of the Press," *The Times Literary Supplement*, London, Sept. 15, 1972.

Parmelee, Maurice: *Criminology*, New York, 1918.

Parsons, Talcott: "The Law and Social Control," in William M. Evan (ed.), *Law and Sociology: Exploratory Essays*, New York, 1962.

Parsons, Talcott: *The Structure of Social Action*, New York, 1968.

Petrazhitsky, L.: *Theory of Law and State*, St. Petersburg, 1909.

Piontkovskii, A. A.: *Uchenie o prestuplenii po sovetskomu ugolovnomu pravu*, Moscow, 1961.

Pollock, Frederick, and William Frederick Maitland: *The History of English Law*, 2d ed., Cambridge, 1898.

Post, A. H.: *Die Grundlagen des Rechts, Leitfaden für den aufbau einer allgemeinen Rechtswissenschaft auf soziologischer Basis*, Oldenburg, 1884.

Pound, Roscoe: *Laws and Morals*, 2d ed., Chapel Hill, N.C., 1924.

Pound, Roscoe: *Outlines of Lectures on Jurisprudence*, 4th ed., Cambridge, Mass., 1928.

Pound, Roscoe: *An Introduction to the Philosophy of Law,* New Haven, Conn., 1965.

Prins, Adolphe: *La défense sociale et les transformation du droit penal,* Bruxelles, 1910.

Proal, Louis: *La Criminalité politique,* Paris, 1895.

Proal, Louis: *Political Crime,* trans. unknown, New York, 1898.

Quetelet, Adolphe: *Sur l'homme et le développement de ses facultés ou essai de physique sociale,* Paris, 1835.

Radbruch, Gustav: *Rechtsphilosophie,* 3d ed., Berlin, 1932.

Radbruch, Gustav: *Mensch im Recht,* 2d ed., Göttingen, 1961.

Radzinowicz, Leon: *A History of English Criminal Law and Its Administration from 1750,* London, 1948–1956.

Radzinowicz, Leon: *Ideology and Crime,* New York, 1966.

Rawls, John: *A Theory of Justice,* Cambridge, Mass., 1971.

Rickert, Heinrich: *System der Philosophie,* Tübingen, 1921.

Riesman, David: "Who Has the Power?", in Reinhard Bendix and Seymour M. Lipset (eds.), *Class, Status and Power,* New York, 1966.

Ross, Alf: *On Law and Justice,* trans. Margaret Dutton, London, 1958.

Rusche, Georg, and Otto Kirchheimer: *Punishment and the Social Structure,* New York, 1939.

Sargent, Lyman Tower: *Contemporary Political Ideologies: A Comparative Analysis,* rev. ed., Homewood, Ill., 1972.

Sariia, P. A.: *A Kommunista erkölcs néhány kérdése,* Budapest, 1951.

Sartre, Jean-Paul: *Being and Nothingness,* trans. Hazel E. Barnes, New York, 1956.

Sauer, Wilhelm: *Allgemeine Strafrechtslehre,* Berlin, 1949.

Schafer, Stephen: "Juvenile Delinquents in 'Convictional Crime,'" *International Annals of Criminology,* 1 (1963): 45–51.

Schafer, Stephen: *The Victim and His Criminal: A Study in Functional Responsibility,* New York, 1968.

Selected Bibliography

SCHAFER, STEPHEN: *Theories in Criminology: Past and Present Philosophies of the Crime Problem*, New York, 1969.

SCHAFER, STEPHEN: "The Concept of the Political Criminal," *The Journal of Criminal Law, Criminology and Police Science*, 62 (1971), 380–387.

SELLIN, THORSTEN: *Culture Conflict and Crime*, New York, 1938.

SETHNA, MINOCHER: *Jurisprudence*, 2d ed., Girgaon-Bombay, 1959.

SHARGORODSKII, M. D., AND N. A. BELIAEV (eds.): *Sovetskoe Ugolovnce Pravo, Obshchaia Chast*, Moscow, 1960.

SORLEY, W. R.: *A History of English Philosophy*, Cambridge, 1920.

SOROKIN, PITIRIM A.: *Social and Cultural Dynamics*, New York, 1937.

SOROKIN, PITIRIM A.: "Sociology of Yesterday, Today, and Tomorrow," *American Sociological Review*, 1965.

STAMMLER, RUDOLF: *Die Lehre von dem richtigen Rechte*, Halle, 1902.

STAMMLER, RUDOLF: *Wirtschaft und Recht nach der materialistischen Geschichtsanfassung*, 5th ed., Leipzig, 1924.

STEINMETZ, S. R.: *Ethnologische Studien zur ersten Entwicklung der Strafe*, Leiden, 1894.

STEPHEN, JAMES FITZJAMES: *A History of the Criminal Law of England*, London, 1883.

STRAUSS, LEO: *The Political Philosophy of Hobbes: Its Basis and Its Genesis*, Chicago, 1963.

STRAUSS, LEO: *Natural Right and History*, Chicago, 1965.

STURSBERG, H.: *Die Zunahme der Vergehen und Verbrechen und ihre Ursachen*, Düsseldorf, 1878.

SUMNER, WILLIAM GRAHAM: *Folkways*, Boston, 1906.

SUTHERLAND, A.: *The Origin and Growth of the Moral Instinct*, London, 1898.

SUTHERLAND, EDWIN H.: *Principles of Criminology*, 3d ed., Chicago, 1939.

TARDE, GABRIEL: *La Criminalité comparée*, Paris, 1890.

TARDE, GABRIEL: "Misère et criminalité," *Revue philosophique*, vol. 29, 1890.

TARDE, GABRIEL: *La Philosophie pénale*, Paris, 1890.

TARNOWSKY, E.: "Les crimes politiques en Russie," *Archives d'anthropologie criminelle*, 12.

THOMASIUS, CHRISTIAN: *Fundamenta Iuris Naturae et Gentium*, Halle, 1705.

TIMASHEFF, NICHOLAS S.: *An Introduction to the Sociology of Law*, Cambridge, Mass., 1939.

TIMASHEFF, NICHOLAS S.: *Sociological Theory: Its Nature and Growth*, 3d ed., New York, 1967.

TÖNNIES, FERDINAND: "Moralstatistik," *Handwörterbuch der Staatswiss.*, 4th ed., Jena, 1925.

TURATI, FILIPPO: *Il delitto e la questione sociale*, Milano, 1883.

VACCARO, M. A.: *Genesi e funzioni delle leggi penali*, Rome, 1889.

VACCARO, M. A.: *Basi del diritto e dello stato*, Torino, 1893.

VÁMBÉRY, RUSZTEM: *Büntetöjog és ethika*, Budapest, 1907.

VECCHIO, GIORGIO DEL: *Philosophy of Law*, trans. T. O. Martin, Washington, D.C., 1953.

Violence, The National Commission on the Causes and Prevention of Violence, "Task Force Reports," among others: Hugh Davis Graham and Ted Robert Gurr, "Violence in America"; Jerome H. Skolnick, "The Politics of Protest"; James F. Kirkham, Sheldon G. Levy, and William J. Crotty, "Assassination and Political Violence," Washington, D.C., 1969.

VISKI, LÁSZLÓ: *Szandékosság és társadalomra veszélyesség*, Budapest, 1959.

WADLER, A.: "Die politische Verbrechen in Russland," *Zeitschrift für das gesamte Strafrechtswissenschaft*, 29.

WAITH, EUGENE M.: *Ideas of Greatness*, London, 1971.

WAKE, C. S.: *The Evolution of Morality*, London, 1878.

WALLACE, GERALD, AND A. D. M. WALKER (eds.): *The Definition of Morality*, London, 1970.

WALZER, MICHAEL: *The Revolution of the Saints: A Study in the Origins of Radical Politics*, Cambridge, Mass., 1965.

Selected Bibliography

WARNOCK, G. J.: *Contemporary Moral Philosophy*, London, 1967.

WEBER, MAX: *Grundriss der Sozialökonomie*, Tübingen, 1922.

WEINSTEIN, MICHAEL A.: *Identity, Power, and Change: Selected Readings in Political Theory*, Glenview, Ill., 1971.

WESTERMARCK, EDWARD: *The Origin and Development of the Moral Ideas*, 2d ed. London, 1912.

WHITELEY, C. H.: "On Defining 'Moral,'" *Analysis*, 1959–1960.

WILLENBÜCHER, N., "Die Strafrechtsphilosophischen Anschauungen Friedrichs des Grossen," *Breslauer Abhandlungen*, 1904.

WINDELBAND, WILHELM: *Die Geschichte der neueren Philosophie*, 6th ed., Leipzig, 1919.

WINES, FREDERICK H.: *Punishment and Reformation*, New York, 1895.

WITTGENSTEIN, LUDWIG: *Philosophical Investigations*, Oxford, 1953.

WITTGENSTEIN, LUDWIG: "Lecture on Ethics," *Philosophical Review*, 1965.

WOLF, ERIC: *Vom Wesen des Täters*, Berlin, 1932.

WOLFGANG, MARVIN E. (ed.): "Patterns of Violence," *The Annals*, 1966.

WOOTTON, BARBARA: *Social Science and Social Pathology*, London, 1959.

Name Index

Name Index

Name Index

Radzinowicz, Leon, 168
Rawls, John, 61, 168
Reckless, Walter C., 100n
Riesman, David, 21, 168
Richard, Earl of Arundel, 38
Richard II, 38
Rickert, Heinrich, 108, 168
Ross, Alf, 45, 168
Rousseau, Jean-Jacques, 149–150
Rusche, Georg, 168

Sargent, Lyman Tower, 168
Sariia, P. A., 168
Sartre, Jean-Paul, 109, 168
Schafer, Stephen, 17n, 22n, 30n,
    31n, 32n, 33n, 39n, 57n, 71n,
    105n, 145n, 146n, 147n, 168–
    169
Schopenhauer, 106
Sellin, Thorsten, 19n, 169
Selznick, Philip, 75n
Seneca, 130
Shakespeare, 90
Shargorodskii, M. D., 26, 165
Skolnick, Jerome H., 132n, 133n
Sorley, W. R., 169
Sorokin, Pitirim A., 169
Spencer, Herbert, 122, 130
Spinoza, Baruch, 100
Stalin, Joseph Dzhugashvili, 9
Stammler, Rudolf, 65, 87–88, 169
Steinmetz, S. R., 93, 169
Stephen, James Fitzjames, 169
Strauss, Leo, 169
Strogovich, M. S., 163
Stursberg, H., 97, 169
Sumner, William Graham, 102,
    169
Sutherland, A., 169
Sutherland, Edwin H., 16, 169

Tarde, Gabriel, 16, 96, 97n, 169–
    170
Tarnowsky, E., 125, 170
Tertullian, 32
Thomas of Mowbray, Earl of Not-
    tingham, 38
Thomas of Woodstock, Duke of
    Gloucester, 38

Thomas, Earl of Warwick, 38
Thucydides, 50
Thomasius, Christian, 170
Timasheff, Nicholas S., 47, 59, 170
Tönnies, Ferdinand, 98n, 170
Tresam, Francis, 154
Truman, Harry S., 136
Turati, Filippo, 170

Utevskii, B. S., 26n

Vaccaro, M. A., 96, 170
Valliant, 32
Vámbéry, Rusztem, 58, 62n, 67,
    91, 94n, 98
Vecchio, Giorgio Del, 67, 170
Verri, Vietro, 94n
Vico, Giambattista, 3
Viski, László, 170
Voltaire, 95

Wadler, A., 125, 170
Waith, Eugene, 52, 53n, 170
Wake, C. S., 94, 170
Walker, A. D. M., 70, 108, 109n,
    170
Wallace, George, 70, 108, 109n,
    170
Walzer, Michael, 92, 170
Warnock, G. J., 71, 171
Washington, George, 9
Webb, Richard, 99
Weber, Max, 45, 46n, 171
Weinstein, Michael, 171
Westermarck, Edward, 46, 59, 171
Whiteley, C. H., 81, 171
Willenbücher, N., 95n, 171
Windelband, Wilhelm, 106, 171
Wines, Frederick H., 98, 171
William the Lion, King, 9
Winter, Thomas, 154
Wittgenstein, Ludwig, 70, 171
Wolf, Eric, 23, 171
Wolfgang, Marvin E., 171
Wootton, Barbara, 171

Xerxes, 39

Zoroaster, 79

Subject Index

177

Subject Index

178